Paris Ontario Book 1 in Colour Photos, Saving Our History One Photo at a Time

Photography
by Barbara Raué
2017

Series Name:
Cruising Ontario

Book 177: Paris Book 1

Cover photo: 36 Broadway Street West, Page 58

Series Name: Cruising Ontario
Saving Our History One Photo at a Time
in colour photos

Books Available in Alphabetical Order:
Aberfoyle, Acton, Alton, Amherstburg, Ancaster, Arthur, Aylmer, Ayr, Bloomingdale, Brantford, Burlington, Caledon, Caledonia, Cambridge, Clifford, Conestogo, Delhi, Dorchester to Aylmer, Drayton, Drumbo, Dryden, Dundas, Eden Mills, Elmira, Elora, Essex, Fergus, Guelph, Hagersville, Hamilton, Hanover, Harriston, Hespeler, Jarvis, Kenora, Kingston, Kingsville, Kitchener, Linwood, Listowel, London, Lucknow, Midland, Mono, Mount Forest, Neustadt, New Hamburg, Niagara-on-the-Lake, Oakville, Orangeville, Orillia, Ottawa, Owen Sound, Palmerston, Penetanguishene, Peterborough, Petrolia, Port Elgin, Preston, Rockwood, Sarnia, Seaforth, Sheffield, Shelburne, Simcoe, Southampton, St. Jacobs, St. Marys, St. Thomas, Stoney Creek, Stratford, Thamesford, Tillsonburg, Waterdown, Waterford, Waterloo, Welland, Wellesley, Windsor, Wingham, Woodstock

Book 157: Brockville
Book 158: Merrickville
Book 159: Smiths Falls
Book 160: Portland, Newboro
Book 161: Westport & Area
Book 162: Perth
Book 163-166: Belleville
Book 167-168: Port Colborne
Book 169: Erin in Colour
Book 170: Goderich in Colour
Book 171: Sault Ste. Marie
Book 172: Lake Superior
Book 173-176: Thunder Bay

Book 177-179: Paris

Other Books by Barbara Raue

Coins of Gold

Arrows, Indians and Love

The Life and Times of Barbara
Volume 1: Inventions That Have Enhanced My Life
Volume 2: Entertainment That I Have Enjoyed
Volume 3: East Coast Trips
Volume 4: Olympics Have Always Intrigued Me
Volume 5: Wonders of the World
Volume 6: Caribbean Cruises We Have Enjoyed
Volume 7: Animals
Volume 8: Storms and Other Major Disasters in My Lifetime
Volume 9: Wars, Terrorist Attacks and Major Disasters

The Cromwell Family Book

Laura Secord Discovered

Daddy Where Are You?

Montana Series
Book 1: Montana Dream
Book 2: Life on the Montana Frontier
Book 3: Montana to Boston and Back
Book 4: Montana Sons Go to War
Book 5: Montana Sons Return From War

Visit Barbara's website to view all of her books
http://barbararaue.ca

Table of Contents

Burwell Street	Page 7
Church Street	Page 11
Dumfries Street	Page 16
Dundas Street West	Page 21
Main Street	Page 23
Washington Street	Page 24
Queen Street	Page 28
Ball Street	Page 30
Arnold Street	Page 31
Grand River Street South	Page 35
King Edward Street	Page 44
Grand River Street North	Page 44
Mechanic Street	Page 54
Broadway Street West	Page 55
Architectural Terms	Page 64
Building Styles	Page 68

Paris

Paris, Ontario is located on the Grand River. It was first settled by Hiram Capron a native of Vermont who, in 1822, emigrated to Norfolk County where he helped to establish one of Upper Canada's earliest iron foundries. He settled here at the Forks of the Grand (where the Grand and Nith Rivers meet) in 1829, divided part of his land into town lots, and in 1830 constructed a grist-mill and named the town after the gypsum deposits that were mined nearby. Gypsum is used to make plaster of Paris. The town of Paris is often referred to as the "cobblestone capital of Canada" because of the many cobblestone buildings that are still standing.

Paris is home to thirteen cobblestone buildings. Mason Levi Boughton inspired Paris' cobblestone technique in the mid to late 1800s. It is estimated that over 14,000 cobblestones were required to build one traditional farmhouse. Each cobblestone is about the size of a sweet potato. Cobblestone architecture refers to the use of cobblestones embedded in mortar to erect walls of houses and commercial buildings.

Levi Boughton was born in Normandale, New York in 1805. He came to Brantford, Ontario in 1835 and in 1838 he moved to Paris. He brought the cobblestone craft to Paris. The cobbles are fist-sized rocks. Boys were paid ten cents a day to walk beside a sled pulled by oxen and throw cobbles turned up by ploughing into the sled. Mortar is laid in horizontal courses with cobbles framed with mortar joints. Cobblestone walls use lime mortar which is a mixture of lime and sand. Lime mortar sets slower, is more elastic and easier to work with than cement-based mortars. Because lime mortars are porous, relatively soft, and have low tensile strength, corners and wall openings in cobblestone structures are strengthened by rectangular blocks of stone called quoins. Window sills and lentils were also reinforced.

Building a cobblestone wall: Working from a foundation of large blocks, an inside wall is laid and the quoins are put in place. A thick bed of mortar is laid between the quoins and individual size sorted cobbles are placed on this mortar bed so that the upper surfaces are roughly horizontal. The cobbles are placed so that they have a gap of two to four centimeters between them. The mason then fills the gap between the stones with mortar. Larger stones extend further back into the mortar trough than the shorter ones. The larger stones help to strengthen the final wall by tying the cobblestone work to the interior wall. After one or two courses of cobblestones are laid, the trough is filled with mortar and waste stone or rocks that are not well sized, shaped or colored for the cobblestone exterior.

Only two or three courses of cobblestones can be laid in one day. If more were attempted, the weight of overlying courses would cause the slow setting mortar of lower courses to bulge and sag. Cobblestones cannot be laid during rain or during freezing weather. Many large cobblestone houses took two to three years to complete.

Jim Percival created scale models of the thirteen cobblestone buildings in Paris.

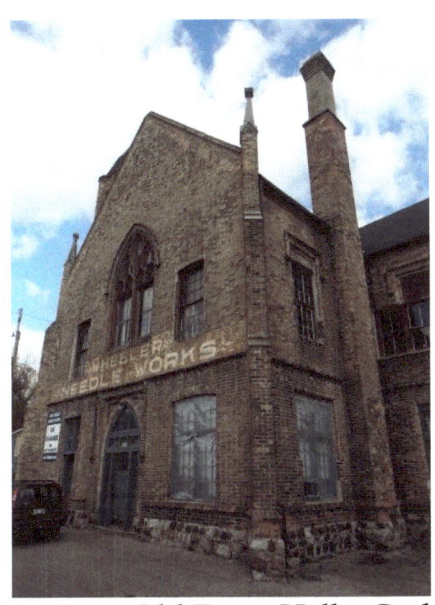

13 Burwell Street - Paris Old Town Hall – Gothic Revival style – 1854 – It had a jail and a second storey opera house. When the town offices were moved, the building was occupied by Wheeler Needle Works.

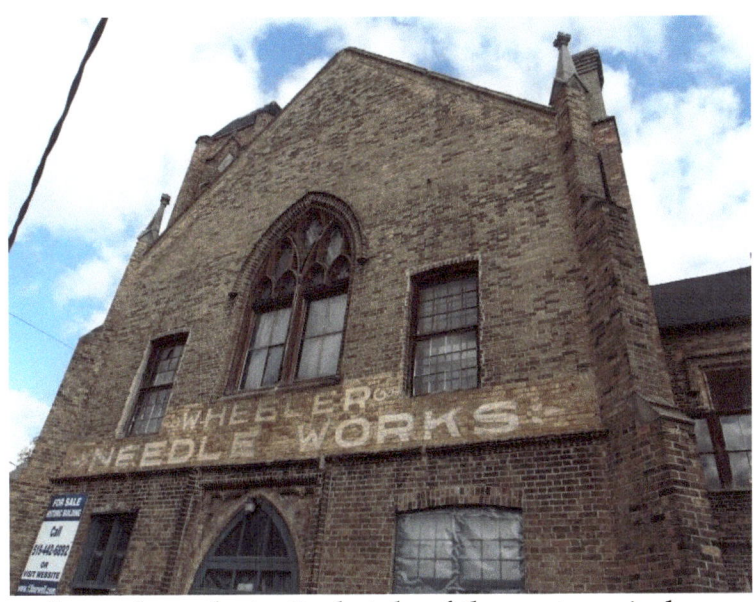

Strongly ecclesiastical style of the centre window

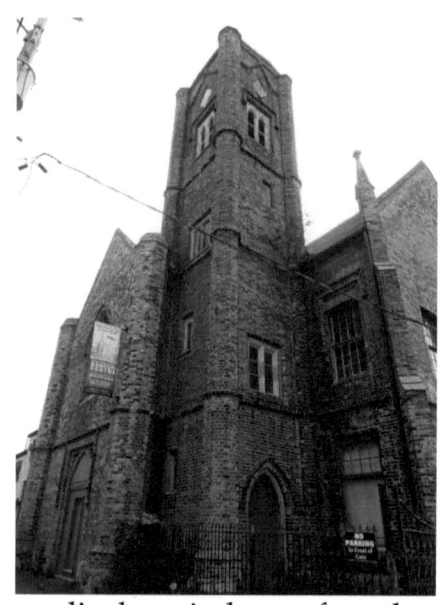

Three-light perpendicular windows of north and south fronts, rectangular moulded frame for the doorway, the octagonal clasping buttresses at the angles of the wings and the tower

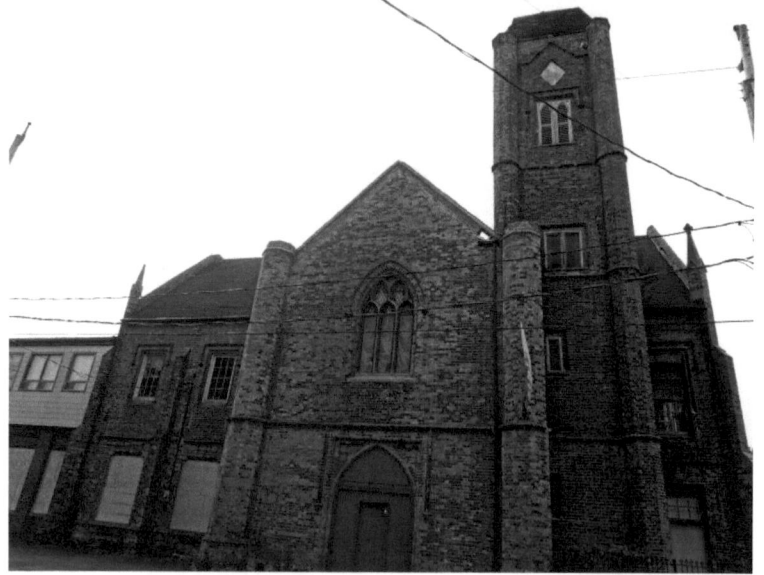

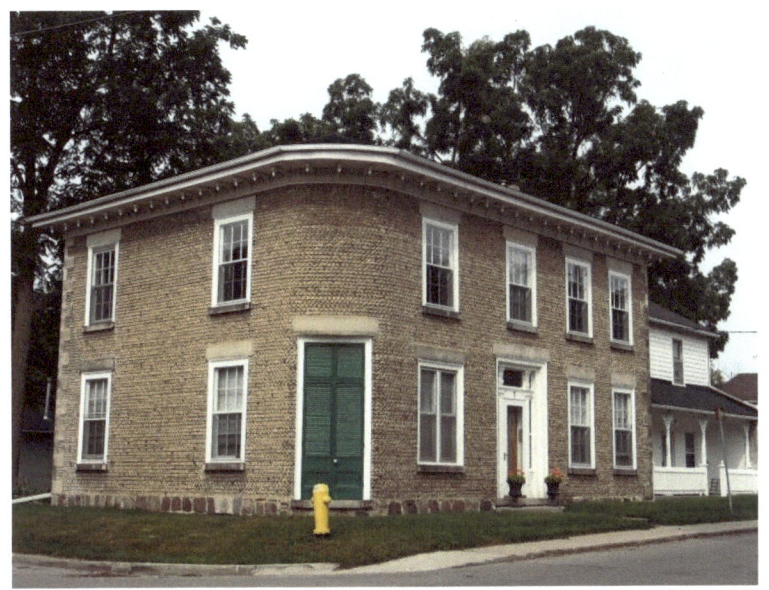

7 Burwell Street – two-storey cobblestone house – 1845-1851 – The rounded corner led to Dr. Sowden's office and dispensary.

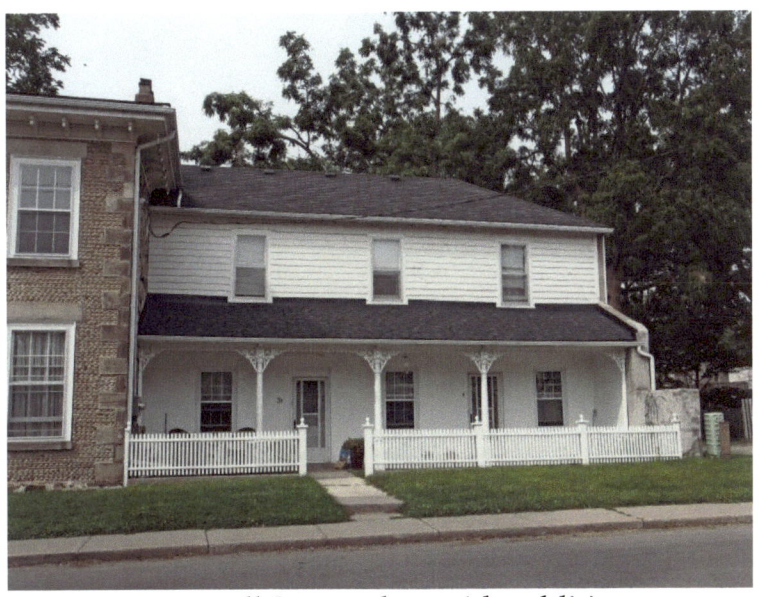

5 Burwell Street – later side addition

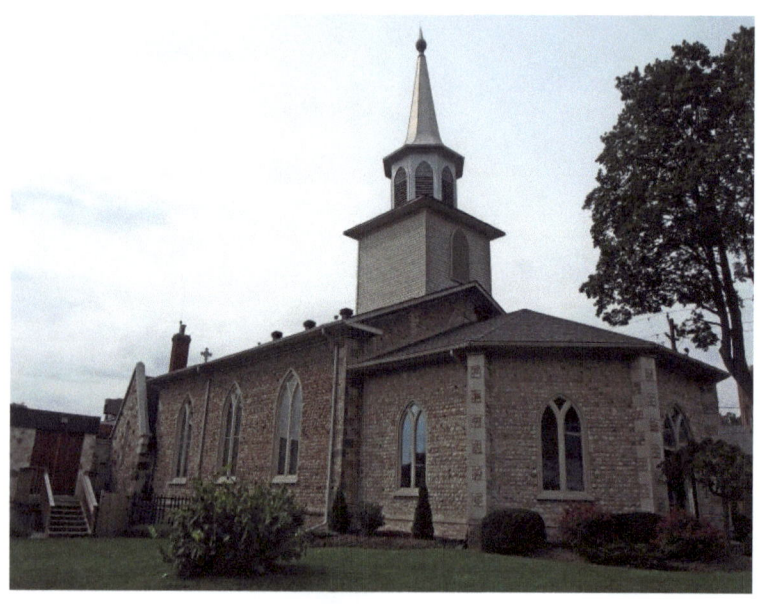

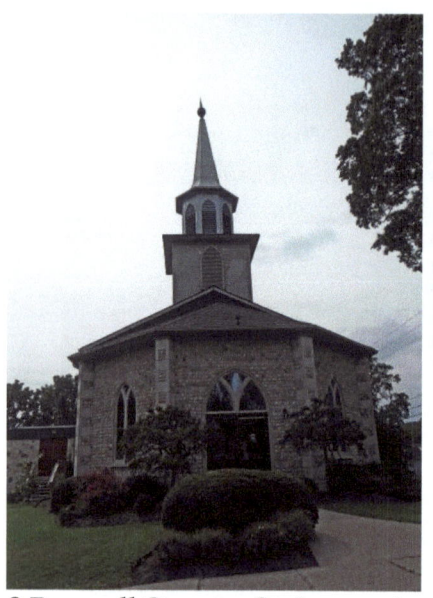
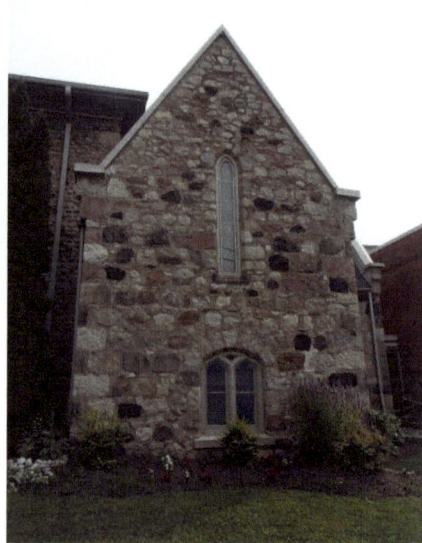

8 Burwell Street – St. James Anglican Church – Gothic Revival – Old part of building, to left, built in 1839 by Levi Boughton, a mason who moved from Normandale, New York and introduced cobblestone-faced masonry. New front section built in 1989.

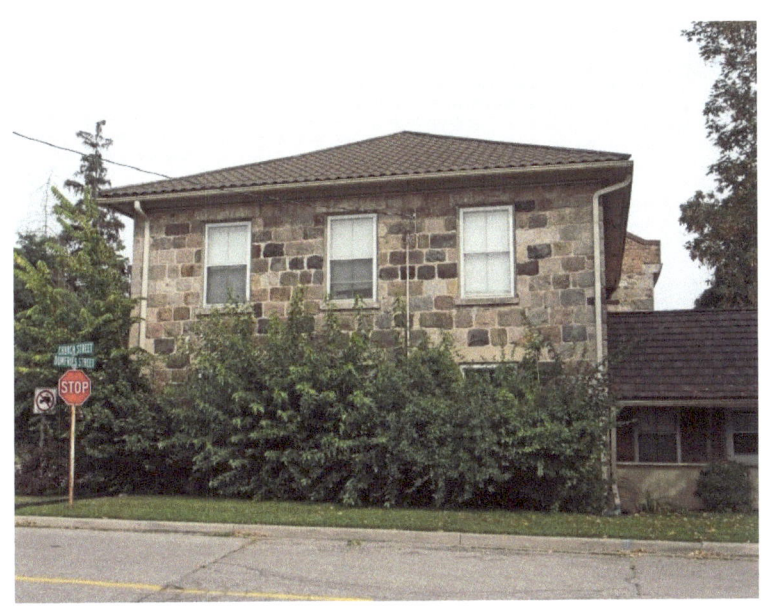

Corner of Church and Dumfries Streets – rubble stone

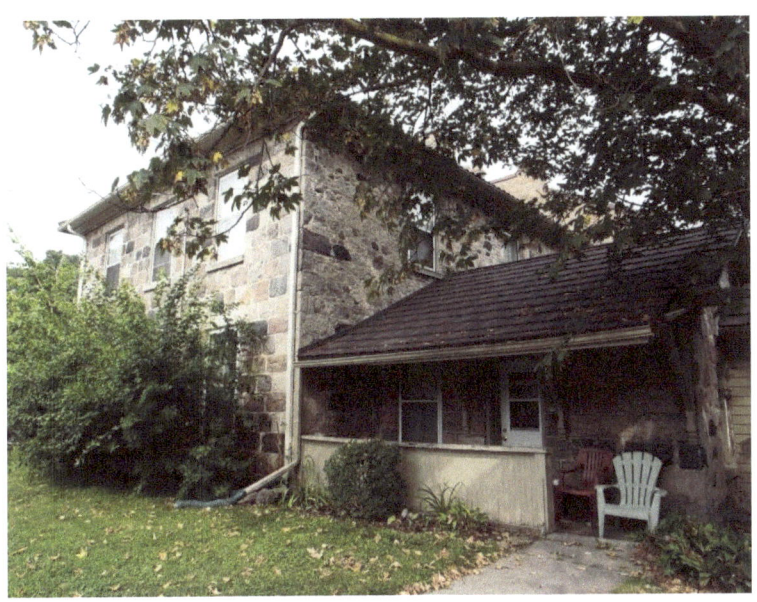

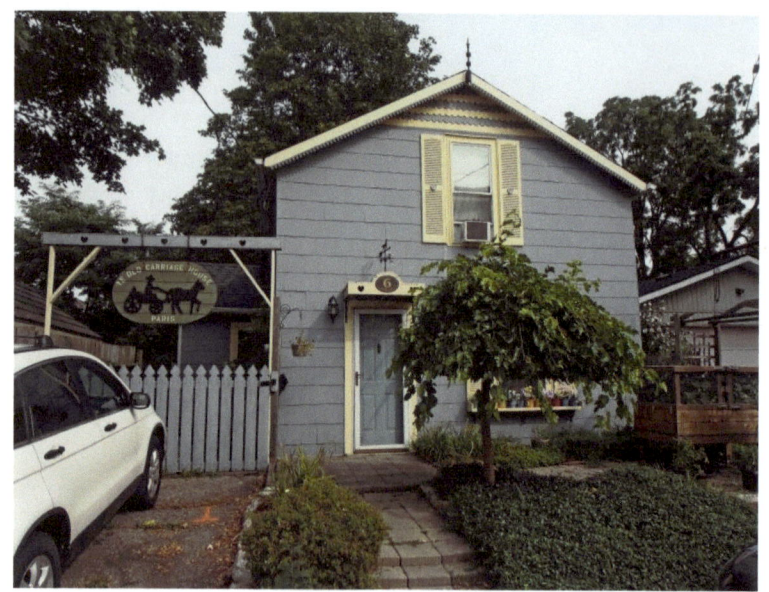

6 Church Street

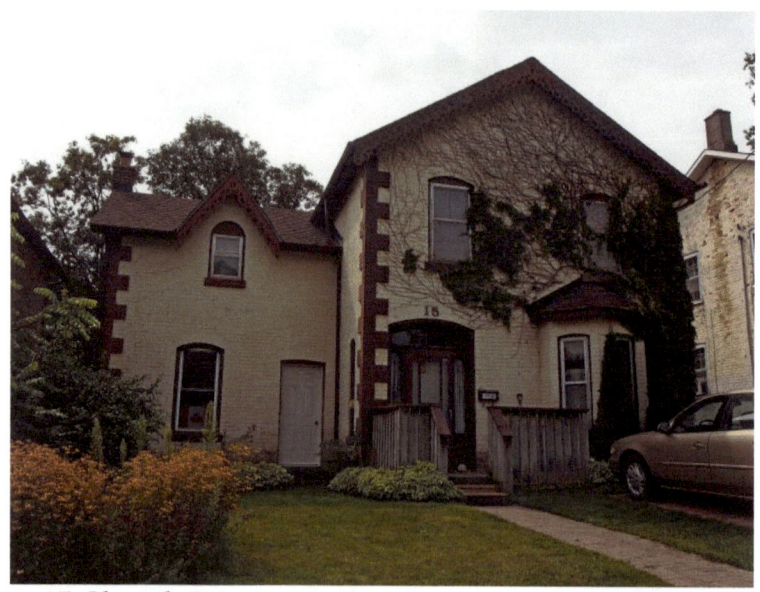

15 Church Street – Gothic Revival – corner quoins

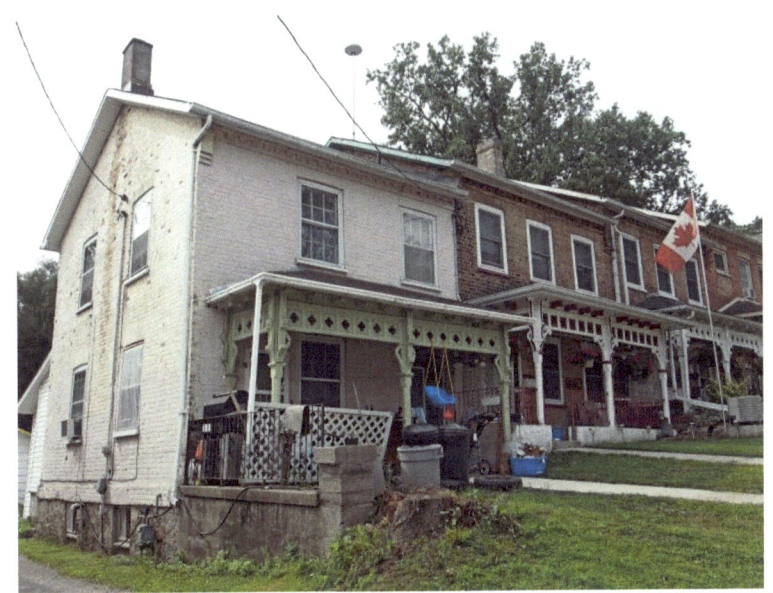

17-19 Church Street

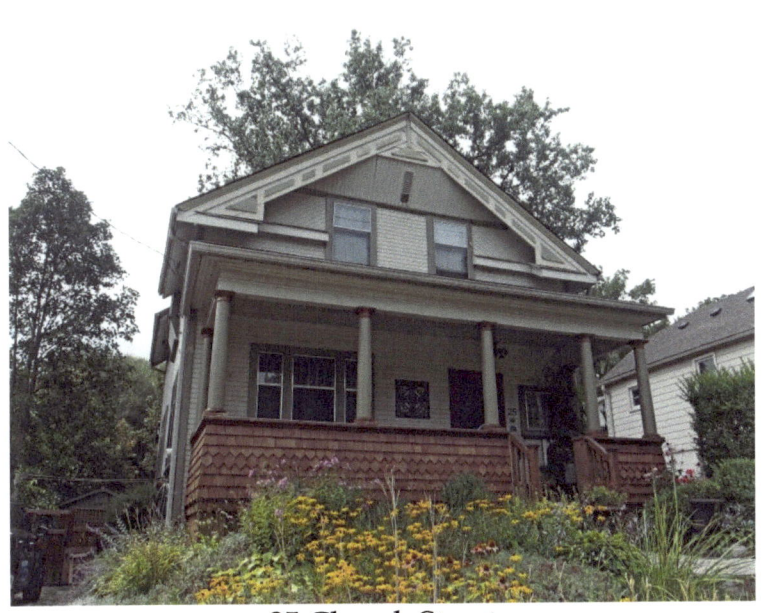

25 Church Street

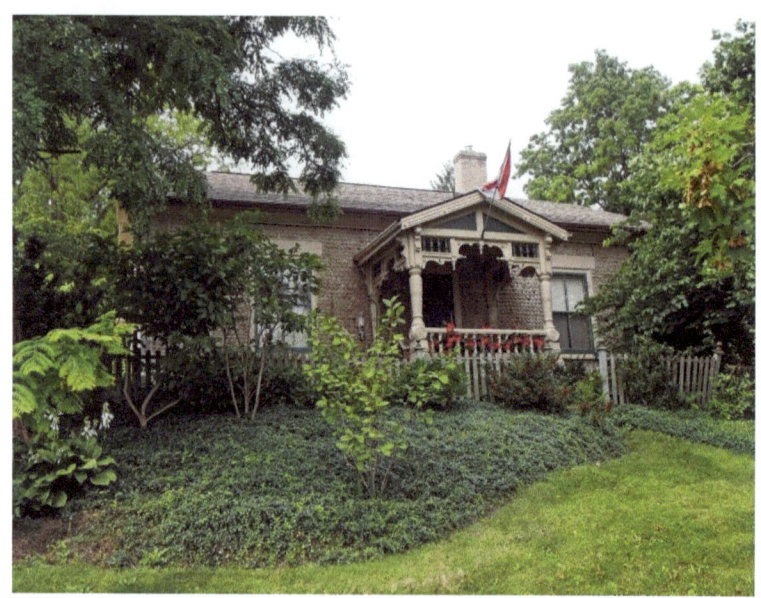

22 Church Street – Dr. Alfred Bosworth and his wife Sarah built their home in 1845. It is in the Queen Anne Regency style and has cobblestones on the front and south facades and cut fieldstones on the other two sides.

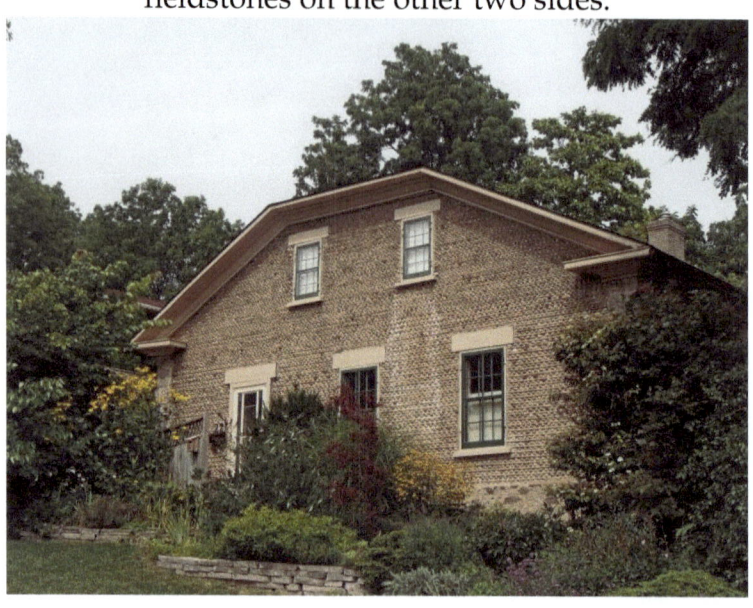

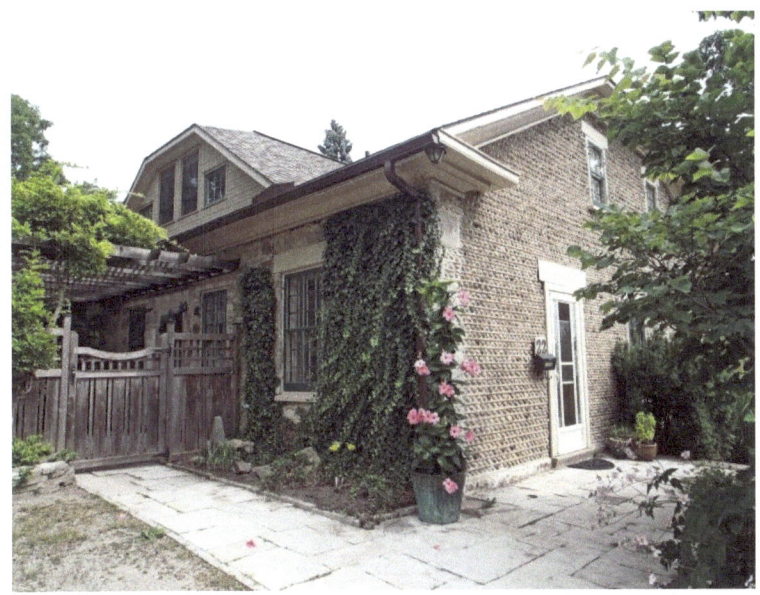

22 Church Street – In 1870, Reverend and Mrs. Thomas Henderson were living in the house. Originally from Scotland, Rev. Henderson wrote to his friends the Bell family and advised them to come to Canada for a healthier environment for their son Alexander Graham Bell.

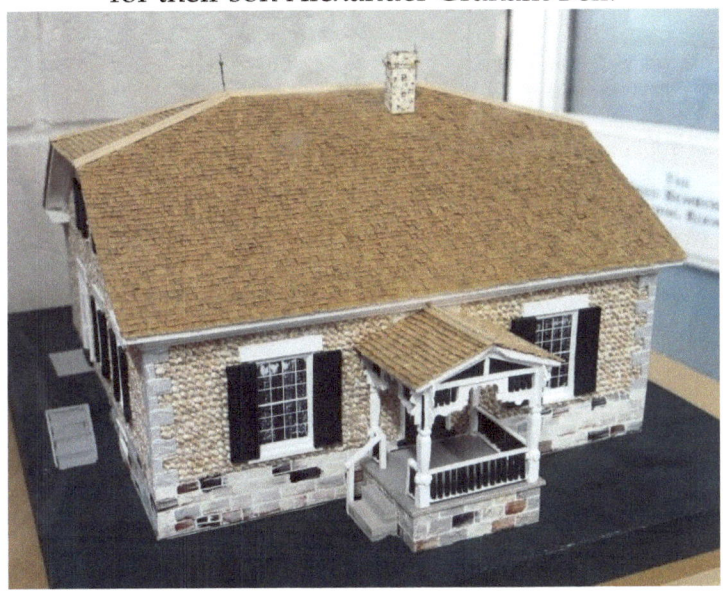

22 Church Street model

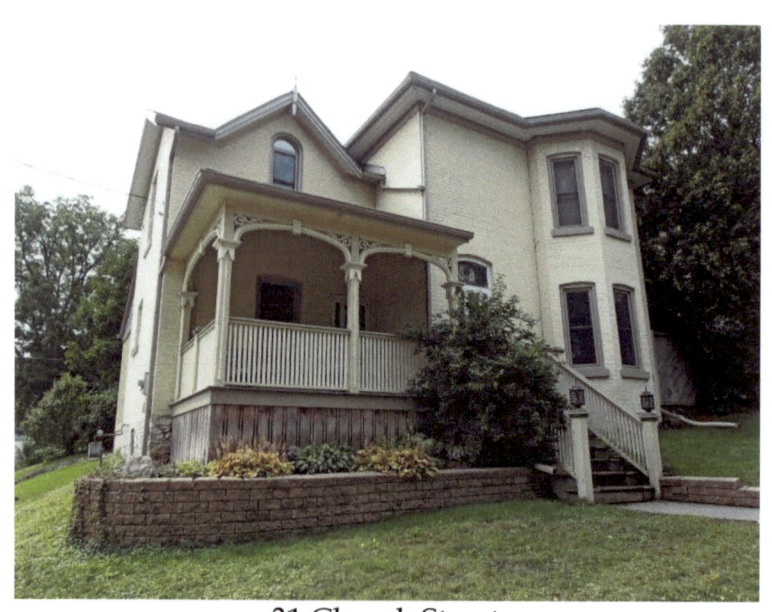
31 Church Street

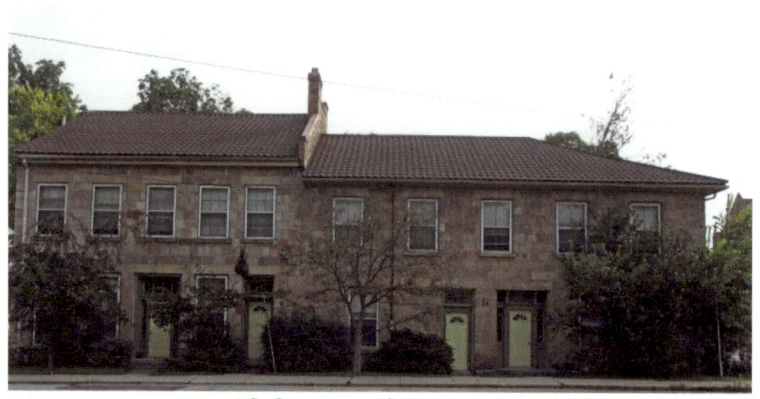
18-24 Dumfries Street

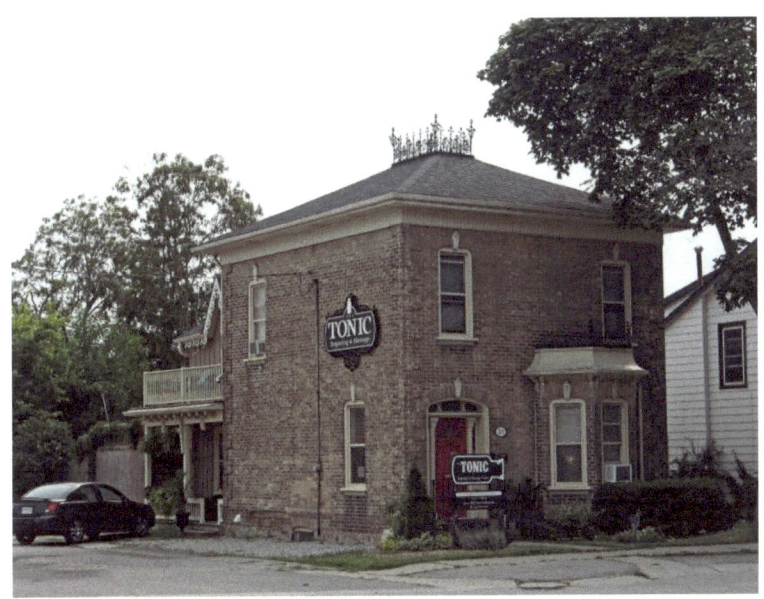

30 Dumfries Street – Italianate, hipped roof with iron cresting widow walk on peak; bay window; back section is Gothic Revival with verge board trim on the gable

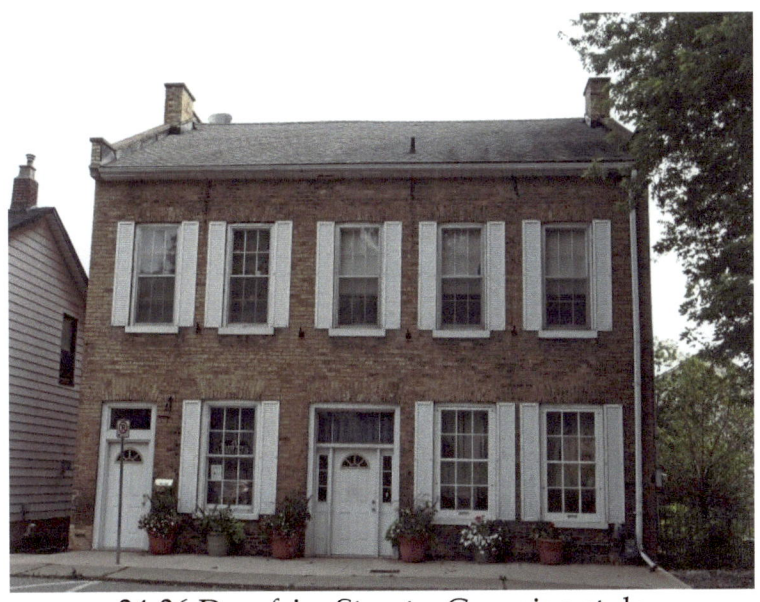

34-36 Dumfries Street – Georgian style

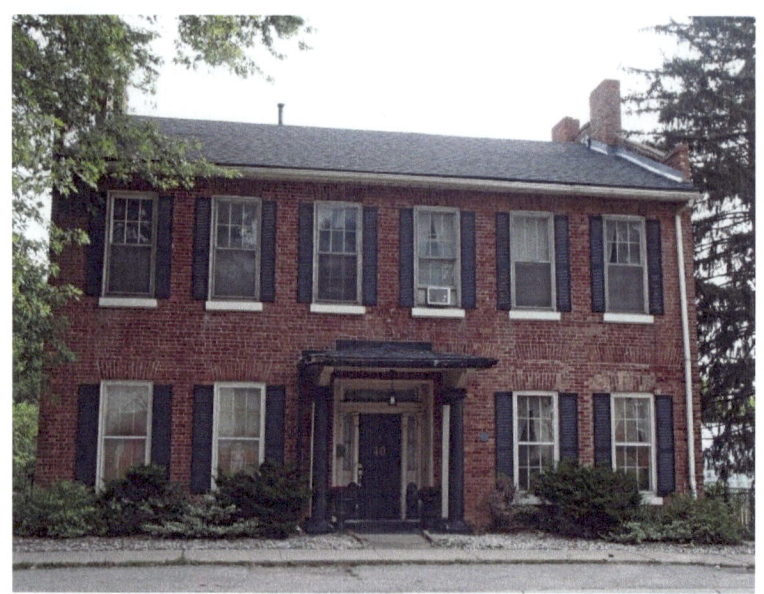

40 Dumfries Street – pre 1841 – Hugh Finlayson was the first mayor of Paris and also the first speaker of the Provincial parliament. He lived in this Georgian red brick house with neo-Classical features.

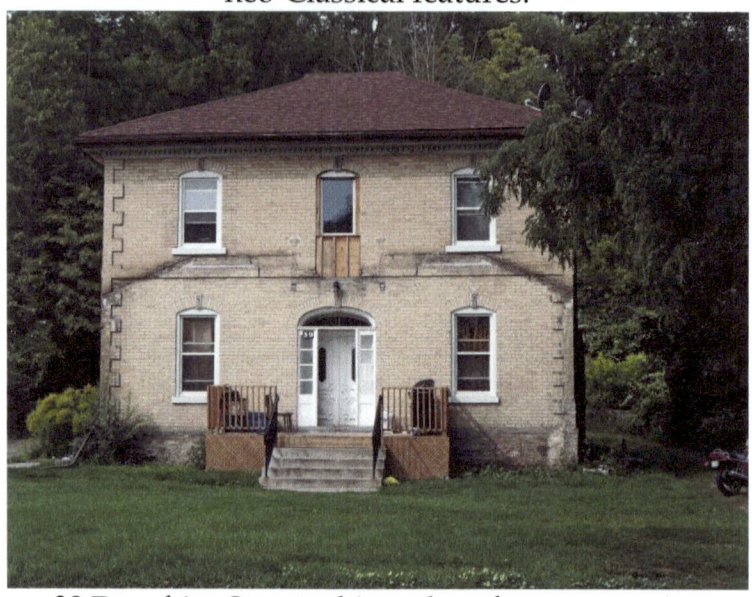

39 Dumfries Street – hipped roof, corner quoins

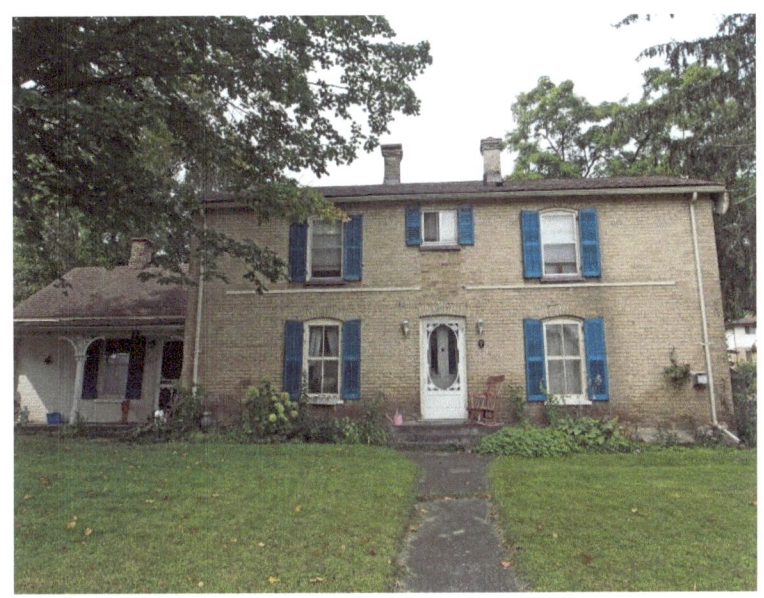

Dumfries Street

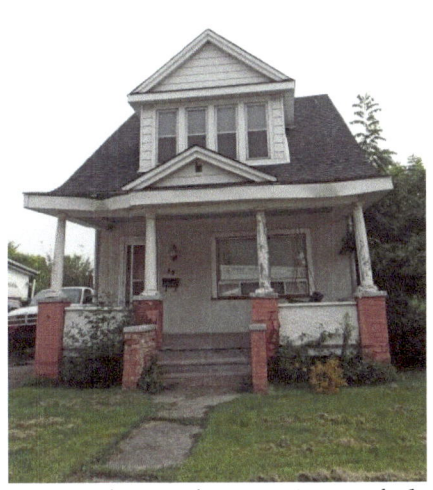

48 Dumfries Street – large dormer in roof above pediment

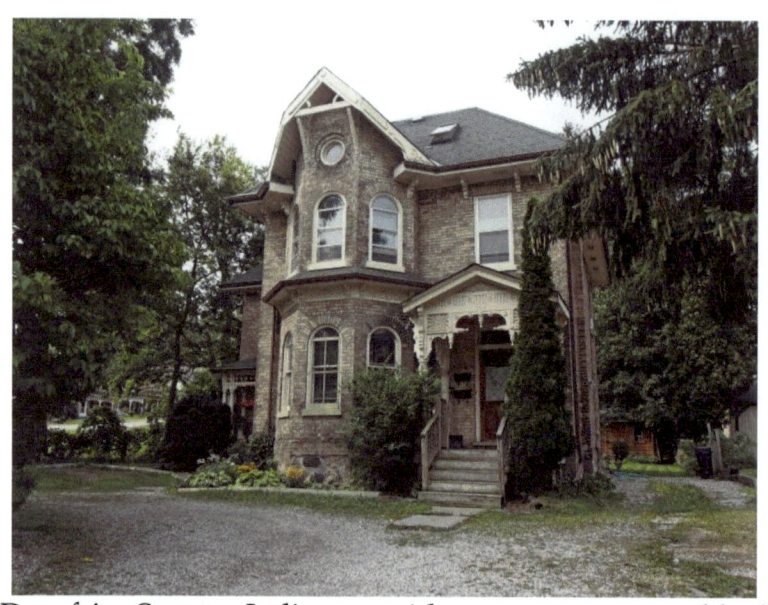

17 Dumfries Street – Italianate with two-storey tower-like bay - Beautiful century home within walking distance to downtown

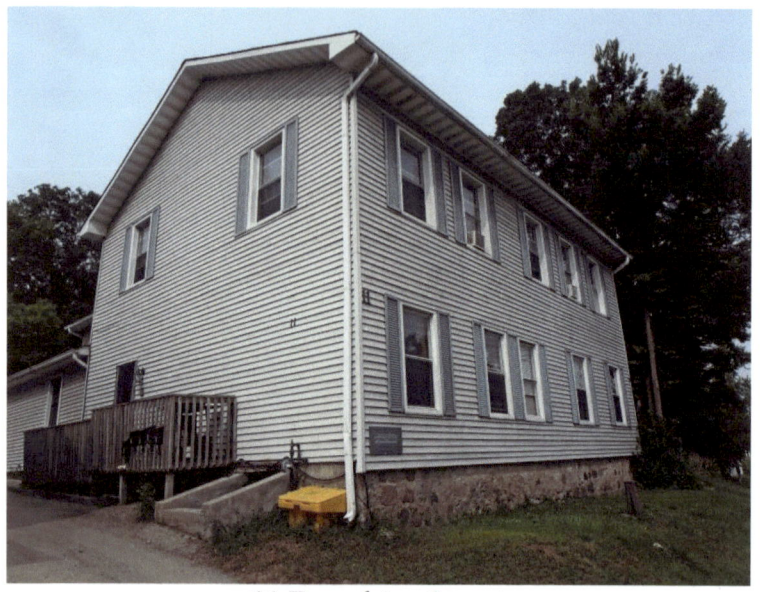

11 Dumfries Street

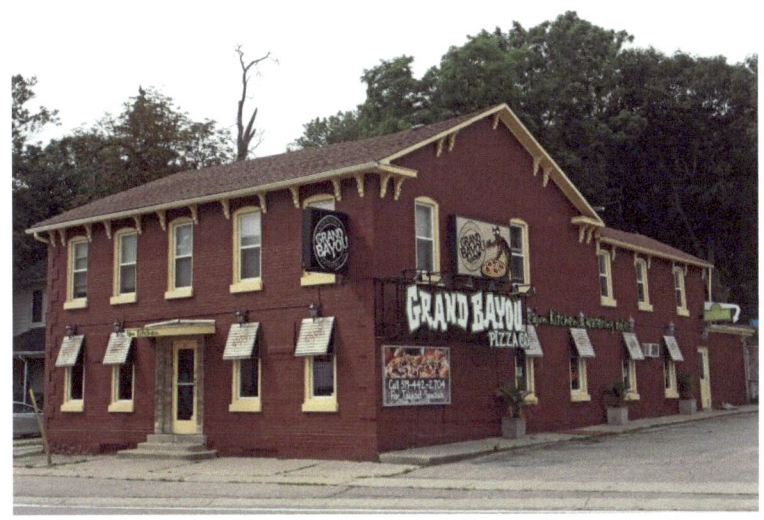

27 Dumfries Street – Grand Bayou Pizza Company – cornice return on gable, cornice brackets

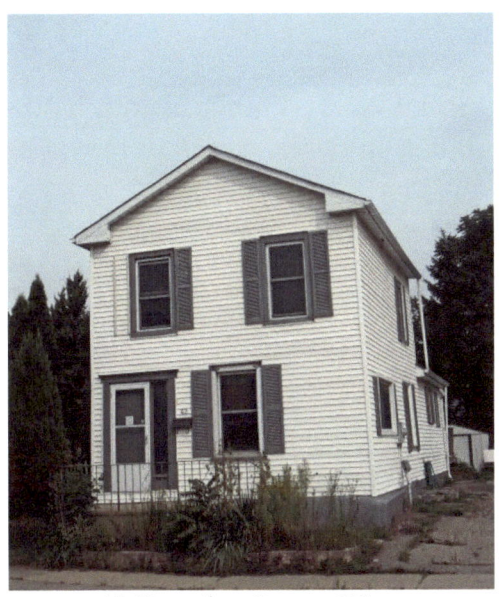

42 Dundas Street West

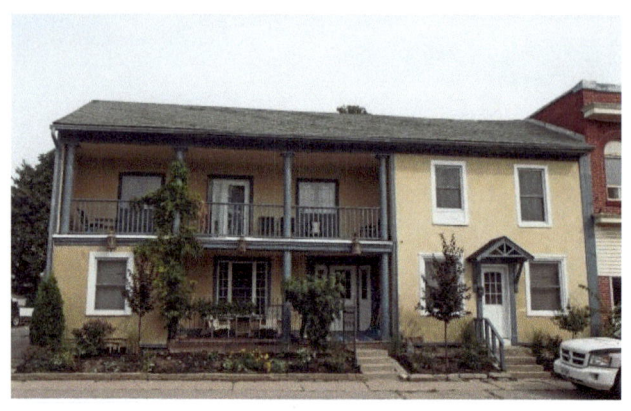

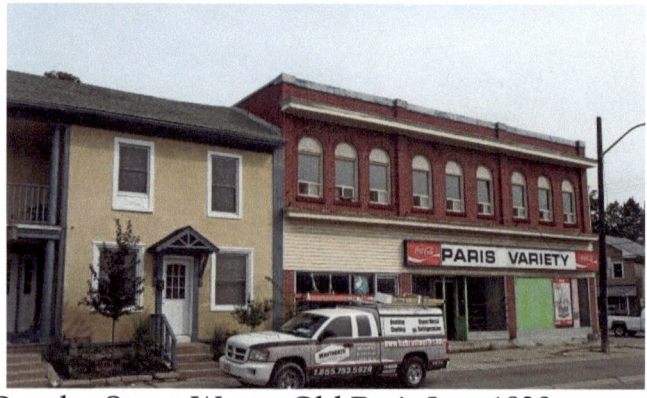

38-40 Dundas Street West – Old Paris Inn, 1830s – was one of the earliest hotels in Paris. French doors on the upstairs balcony led to a ballroom.

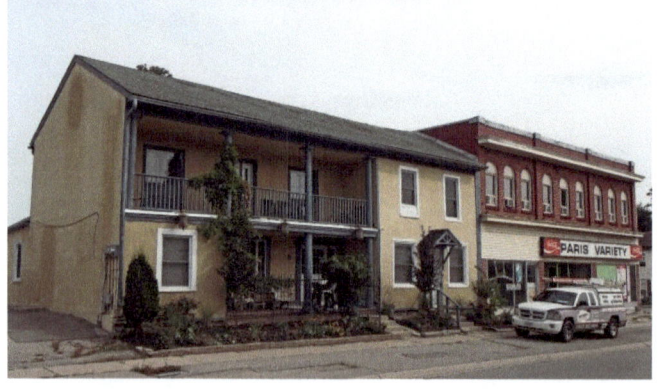

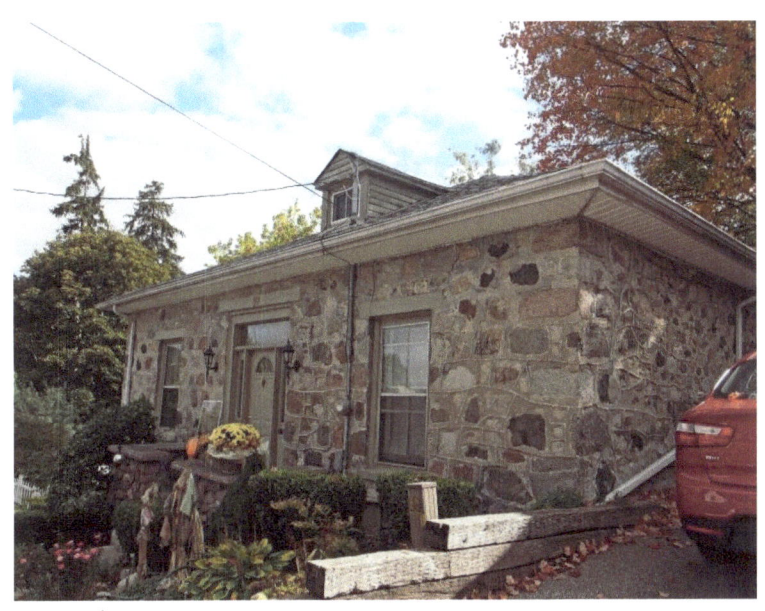

57 Main Street – stone Regency Cottage, dormer in attic

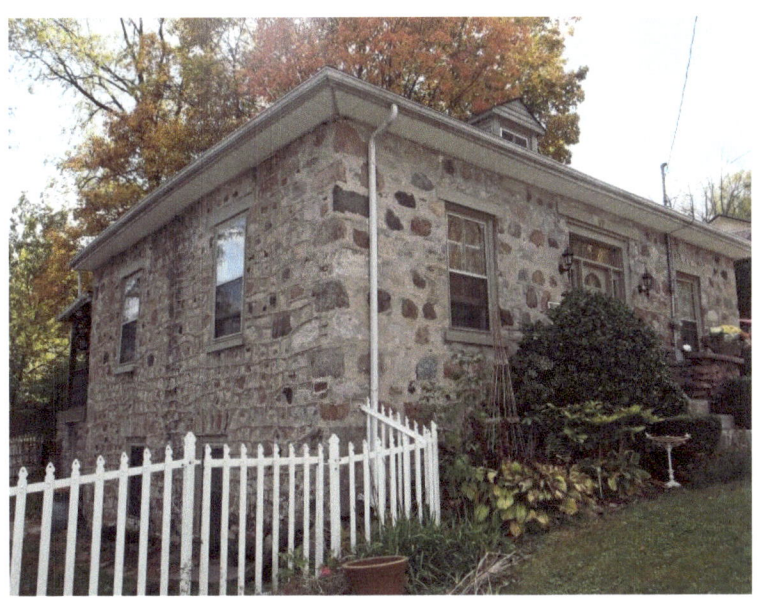

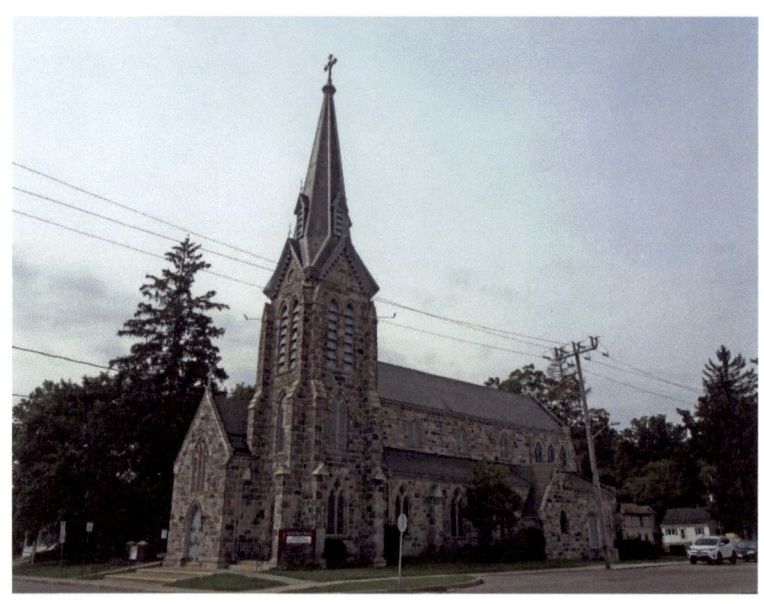

17 Washington Street - Sacred Heart Church – dichromatic tile work on the spire, stone

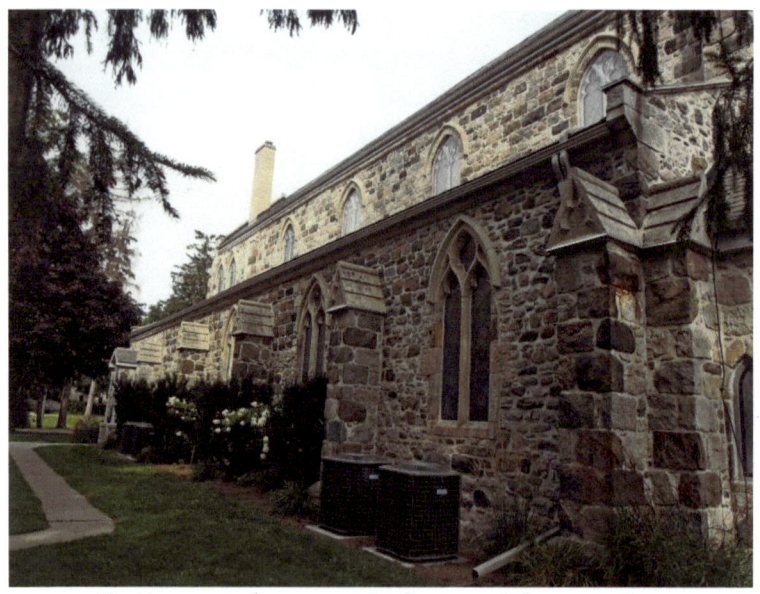

Buttresses, lancet windows with muntins

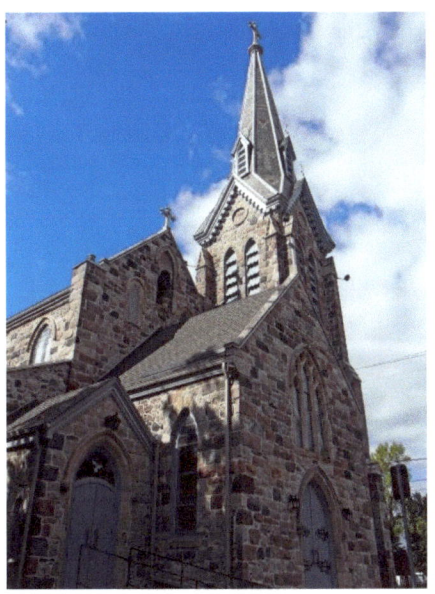

Stone, slate and stained glass combined in a splendid Gothic fashion - 1857

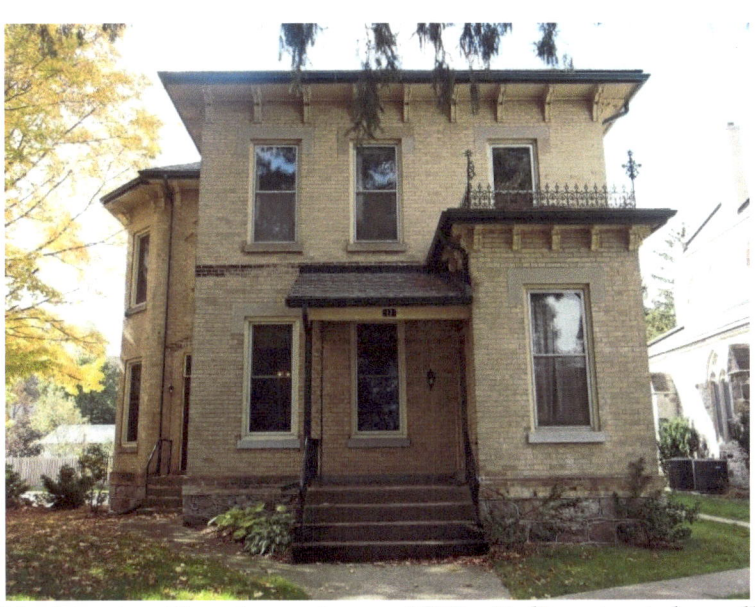

17 Washington Street – rectory – 1875 - Italianate style, yellow brick, iron cresting above square bay window, single cornice brackets

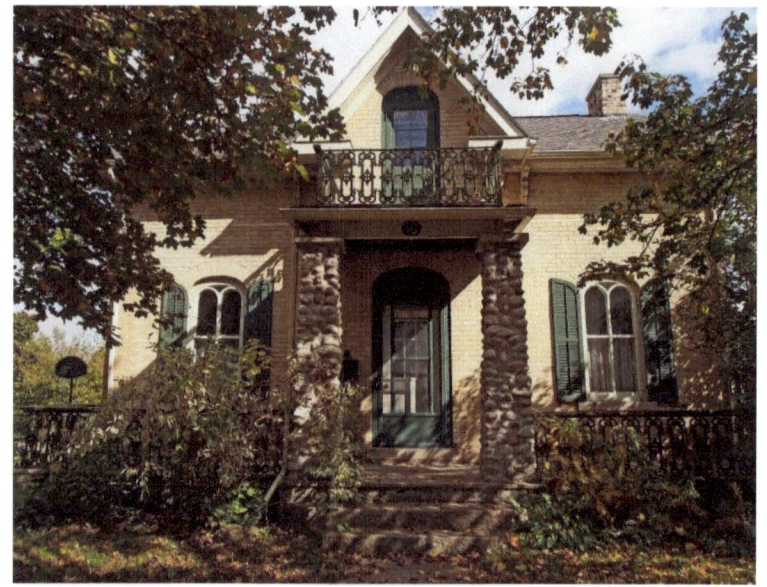

16 Washington Street – Gothic Revival, yellow brick, iron cresting above door, cornice return on gable, cobblestone pillars

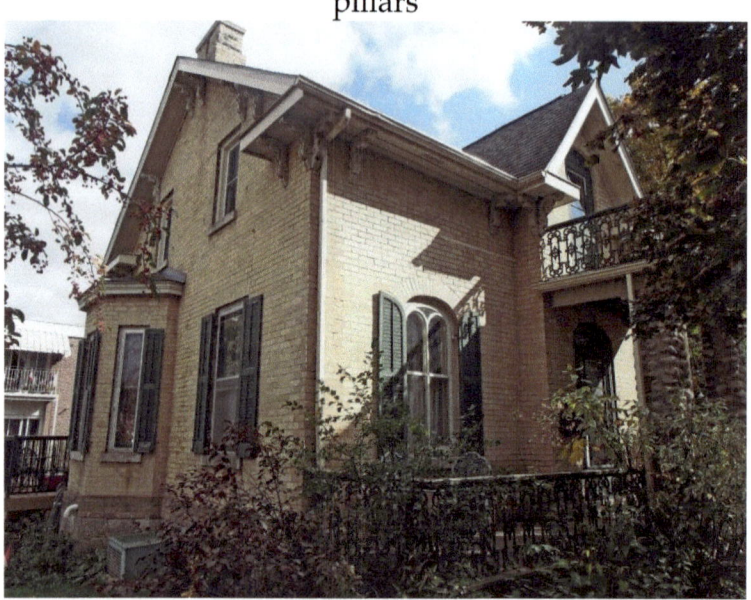

Bay window

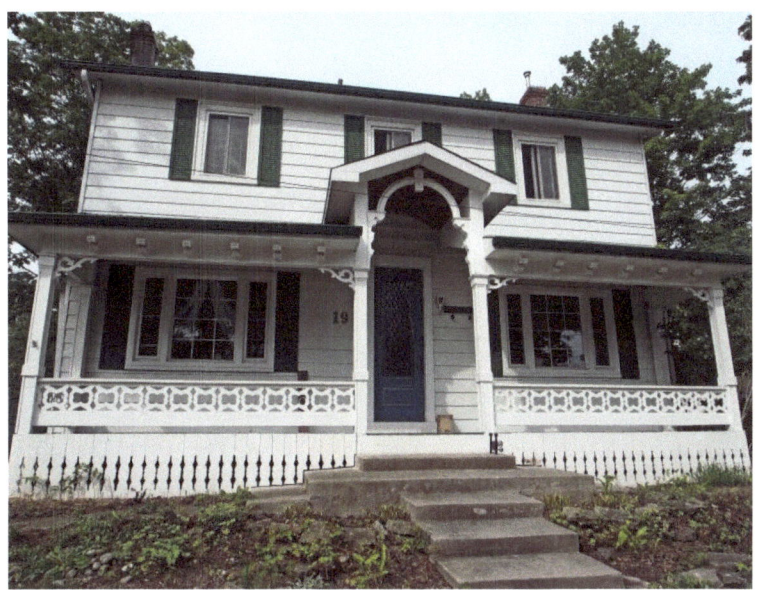

19 Washington Street – Georgian style

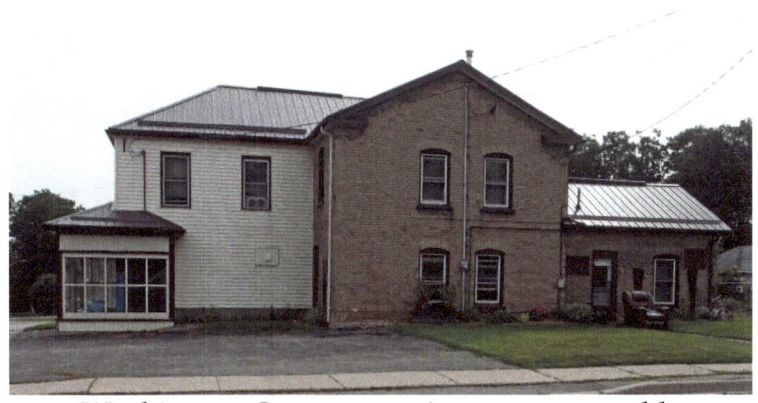

Washington Street – cornice return on gable

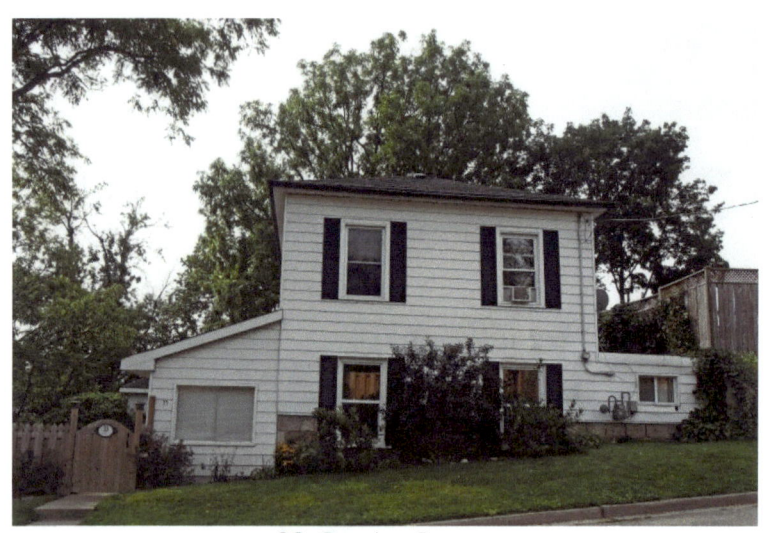

33 Queen Street

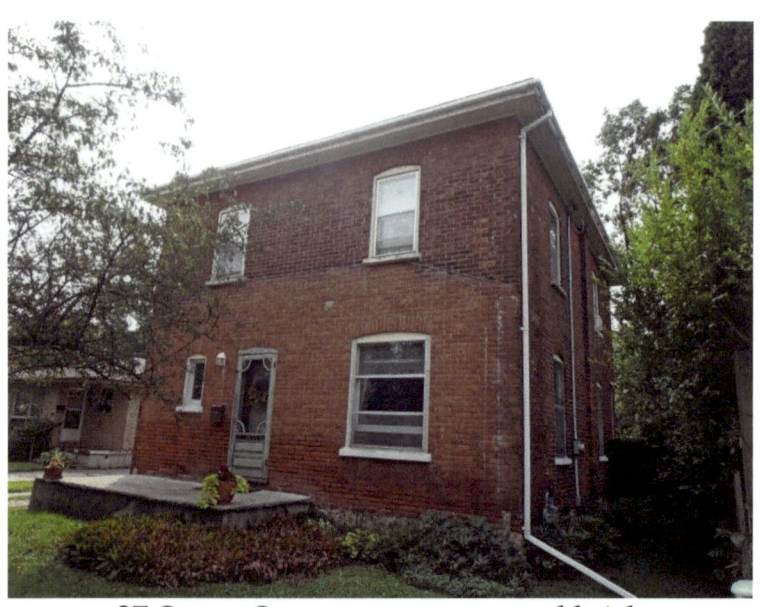

27 Queen Street – two-storey red brick

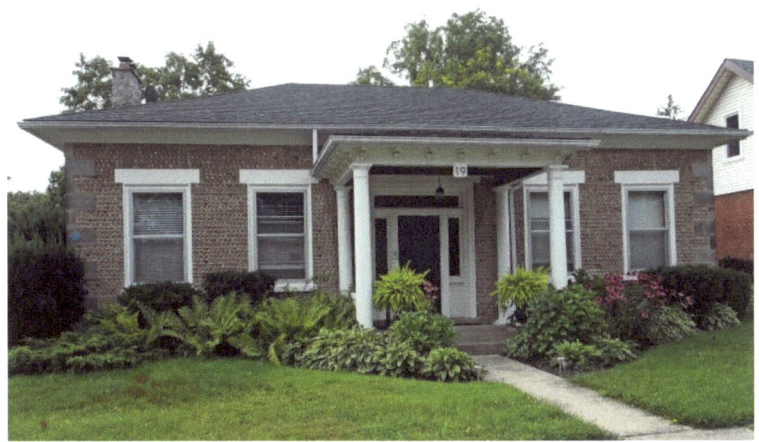

19 Queen Street – Levi Boughton's house is an Ontario cottage is simple and elegant. It looks small but it has twelve foot ceilings. The exterior has cobblestone walls on three sides. The cobblestones are small and evenly matched in size and color. The Boughtons had sixteen children and three of them became masons and plasterers. Under the low pitched roof is nested the plastered and painted attic with a height of less than five feet at the peak – sleeping quarters for the children.

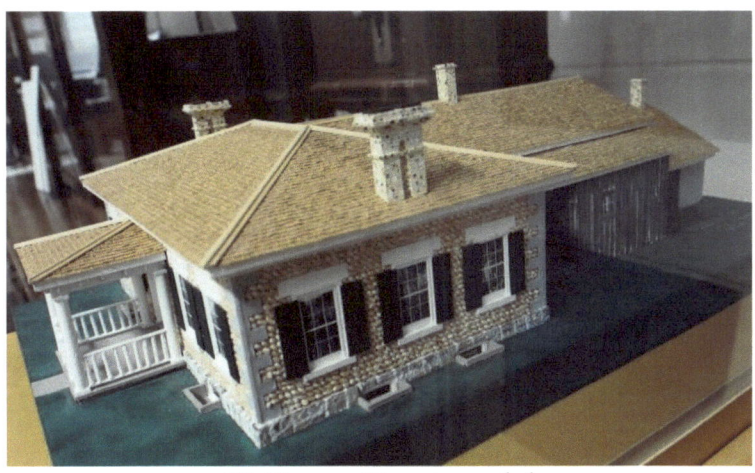

19 Queen Street model

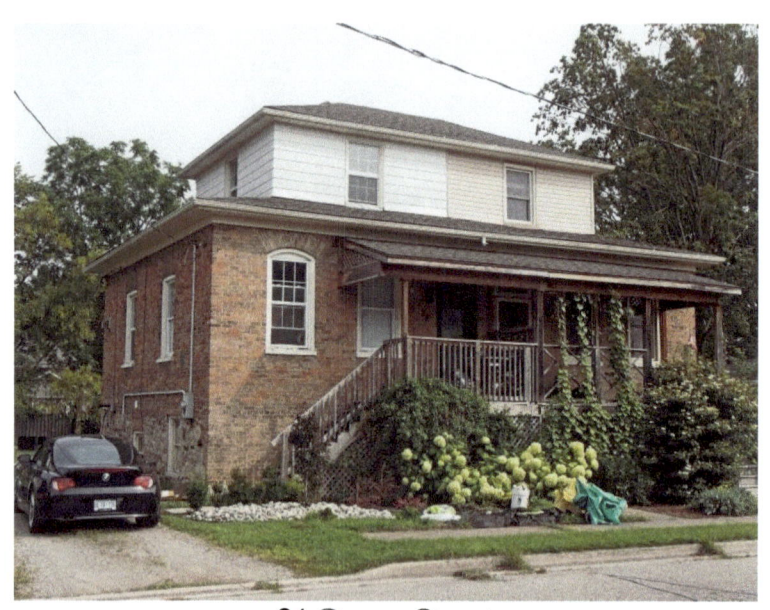

24 Queen Street

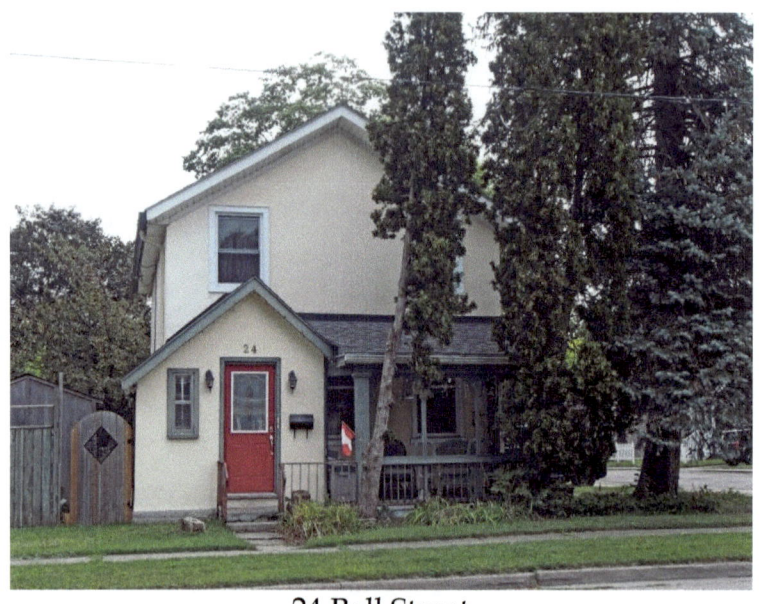

24 Ball Street

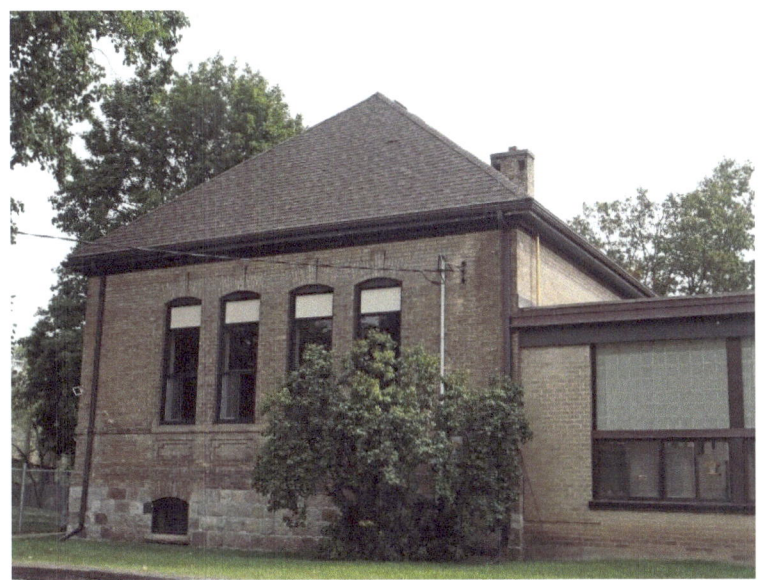

2 Ball Street – Montessori Children's Academy – stone basement

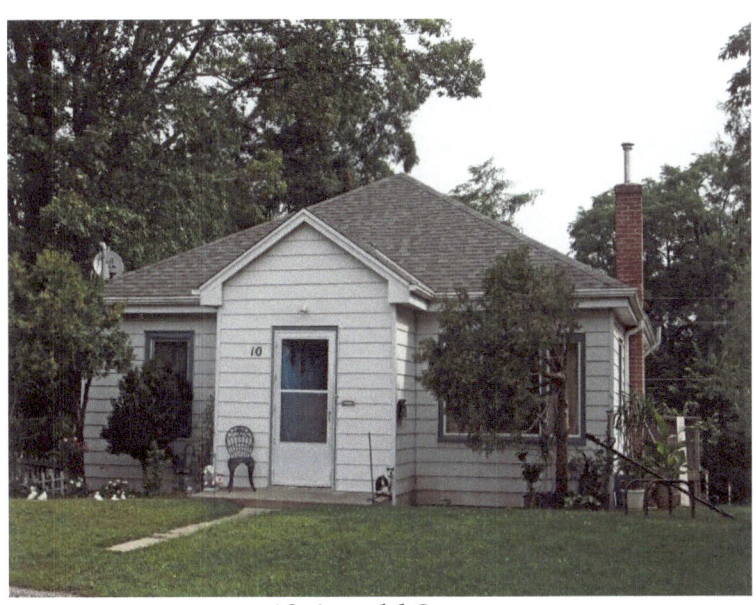

10 Arnold Street

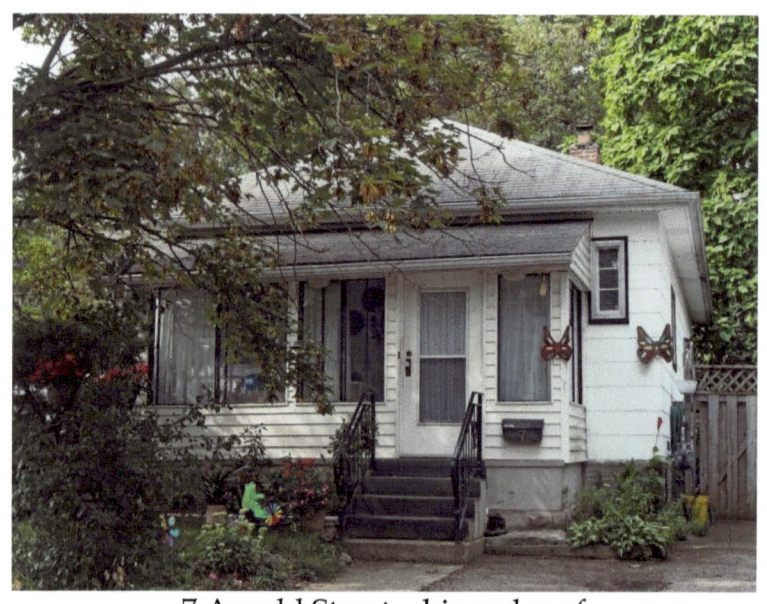

7 Arnold Street – hipped roof

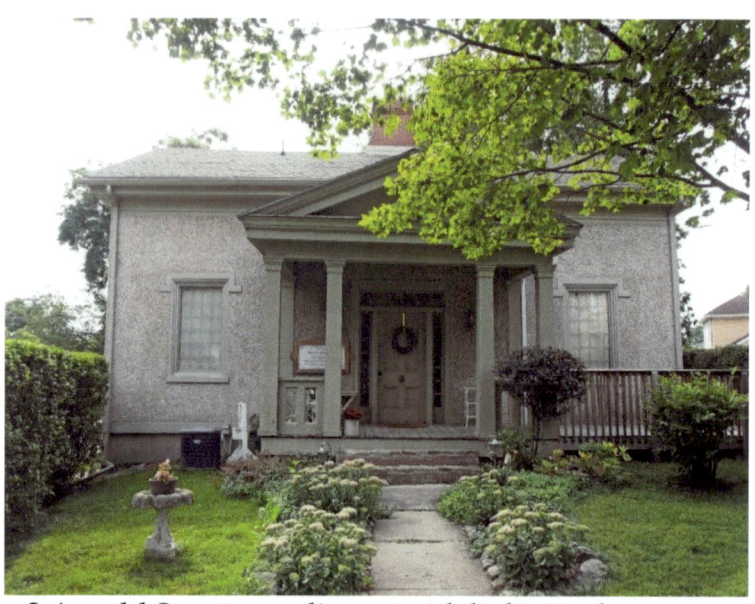

2 Arnold Street – pediment, sidelights and transom

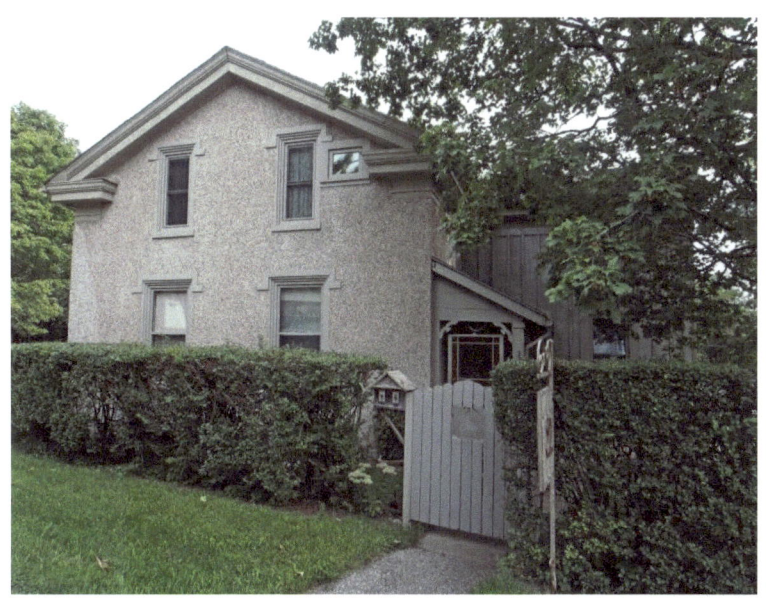

2 Arnold Street – Charles Arnold House – 1840s – stucco house with a cobblestone foundation

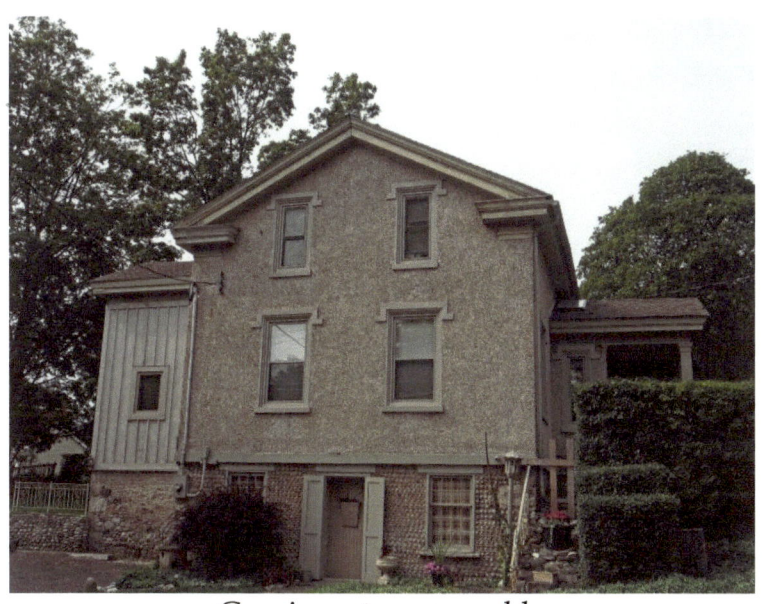

Cornice return on gable

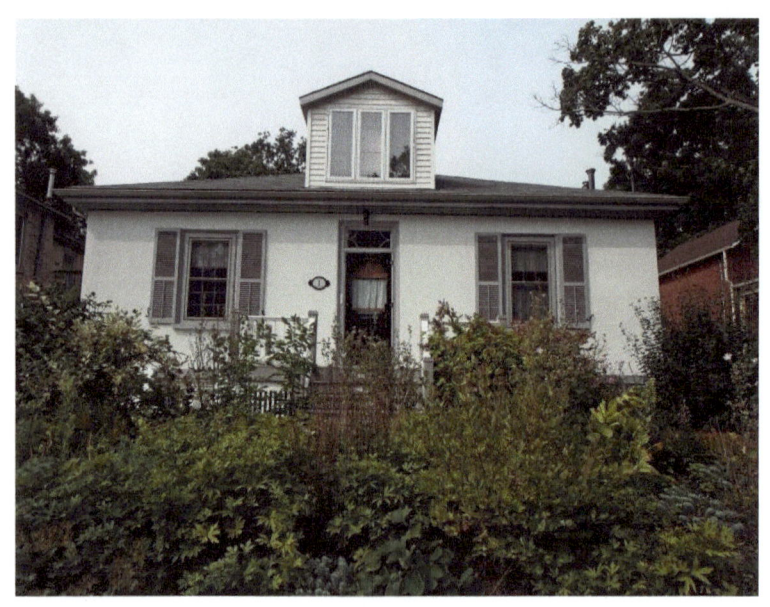

1 Arnold Street - dormer

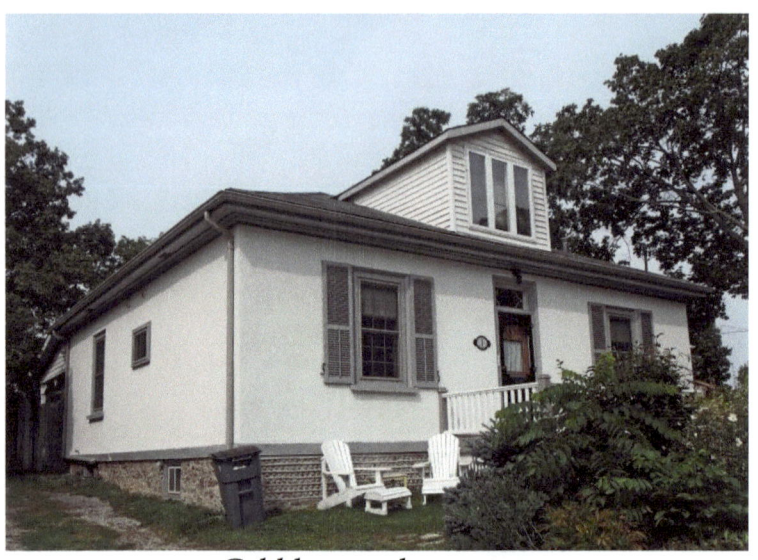

Cobblestone basement

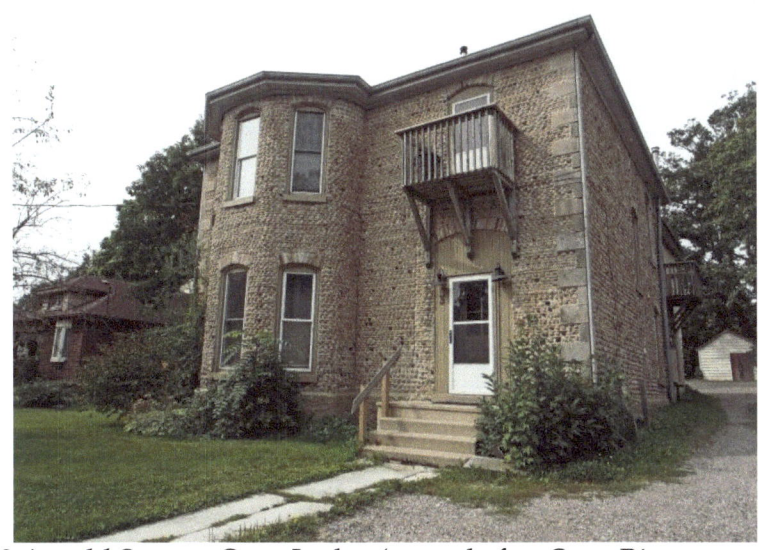

3 Arnold Street – Ouse Lodge (named after Ouse River – now Grand River) – early 1840s - Italianate cobblestone, two-storey bay window, second floor balcony, corner quoins – built by Levi Boughton as the Anglican Rectory for Rev. William Morse. Morse was also a musician and the house had a pipe organ.

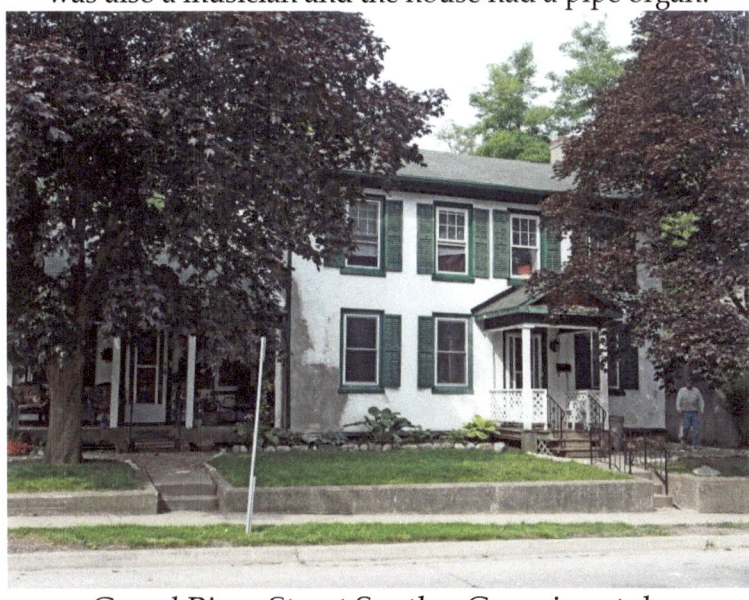

Grand River Street South – Georgian style

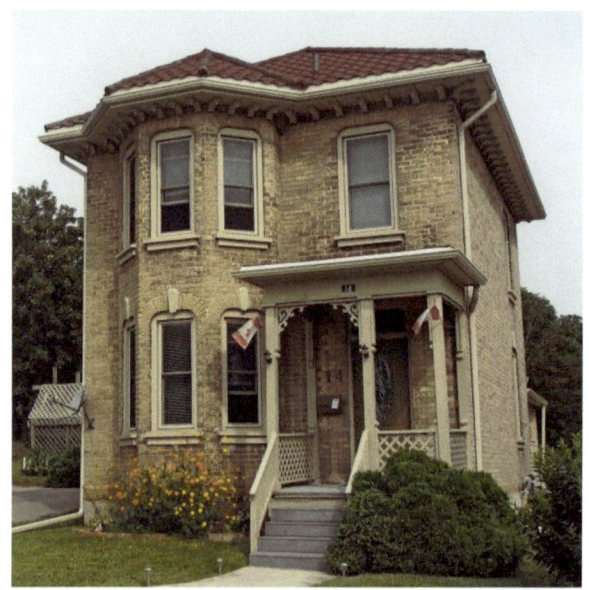

14 Grand River Street South - yellow brick, voussoirs and keystones, two-storey bay window, cornice brackets

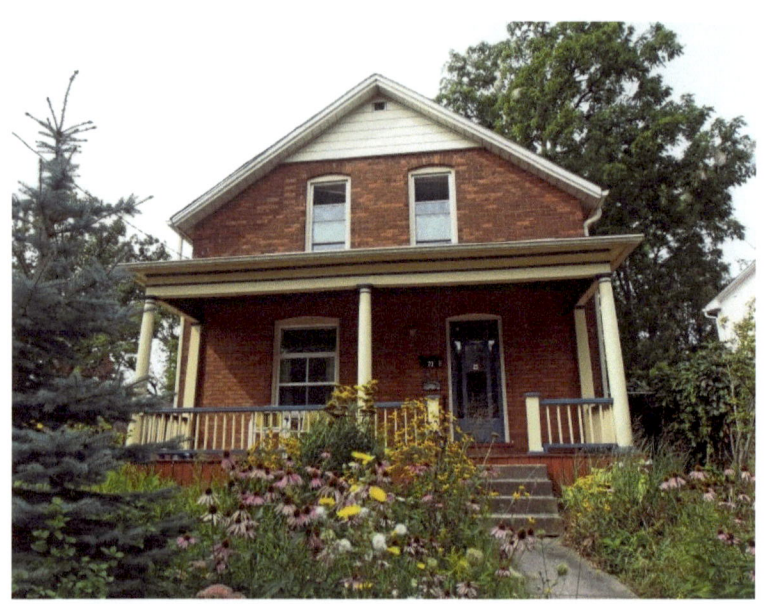

73 Grand River Street South – Edwardian

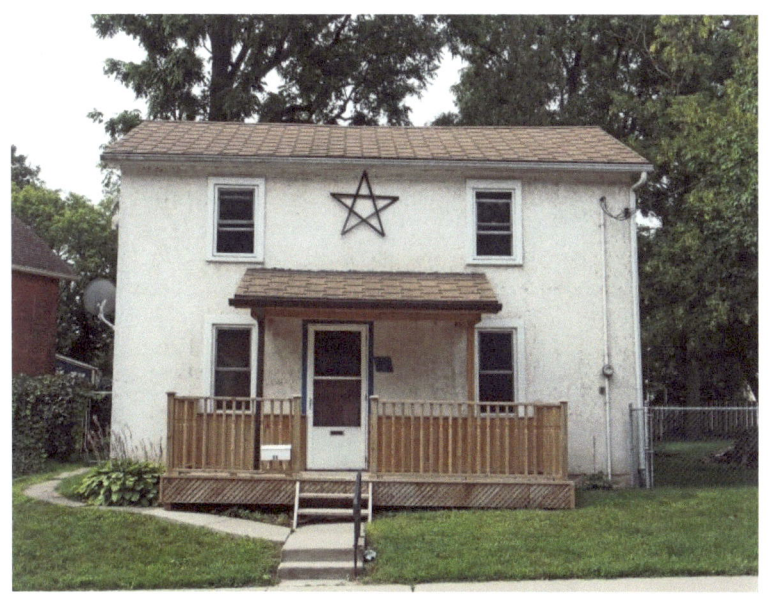

71 Grand River Street South

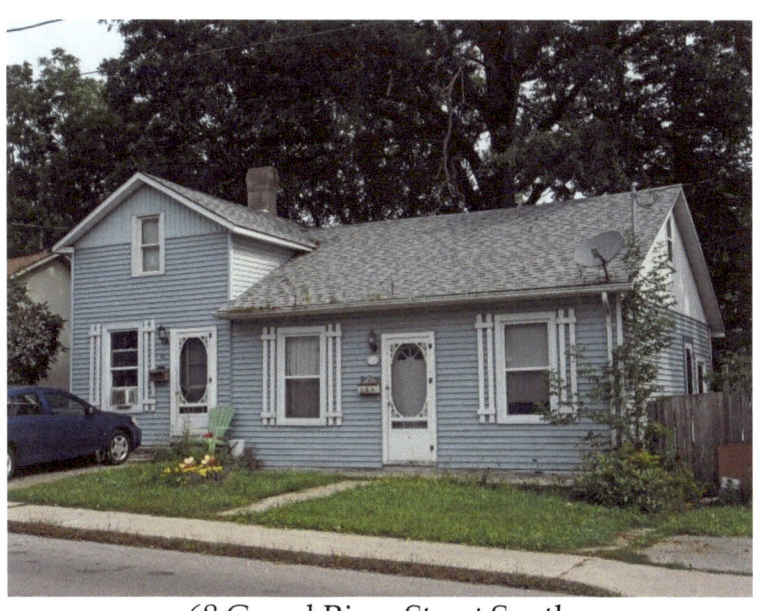

68 Grand River Street South

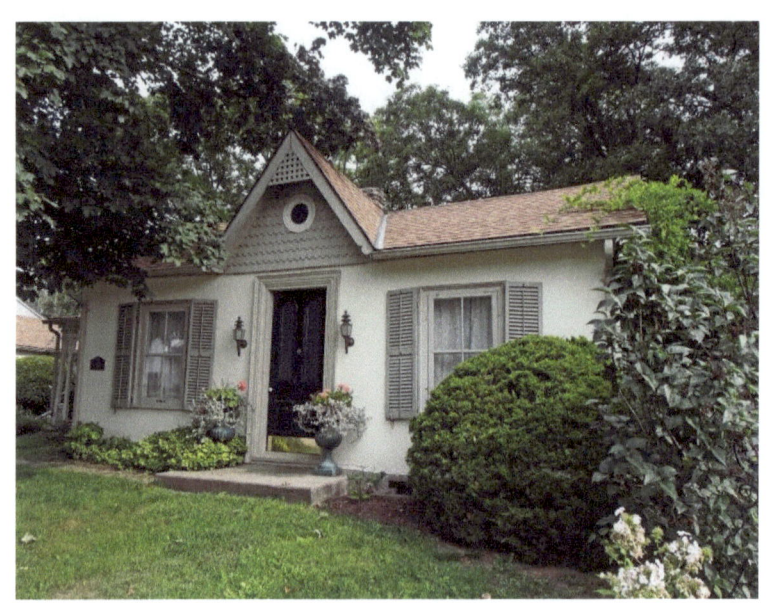

66 Grand River Street South

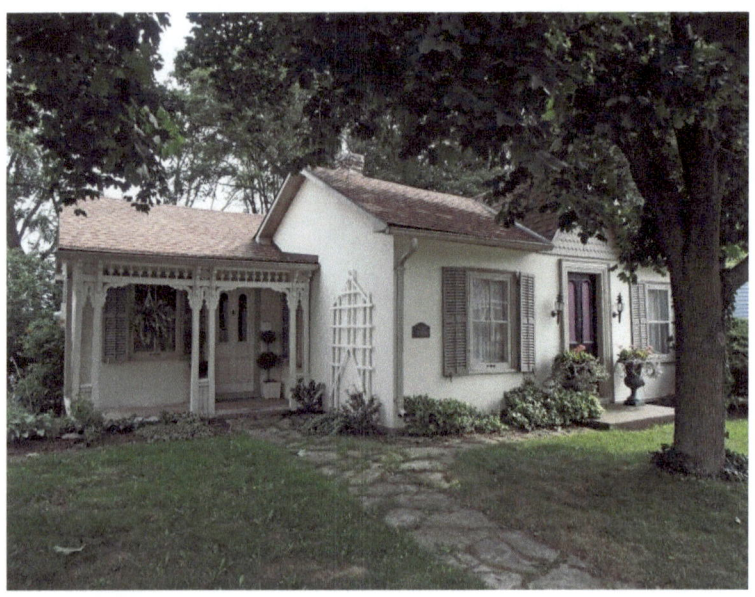

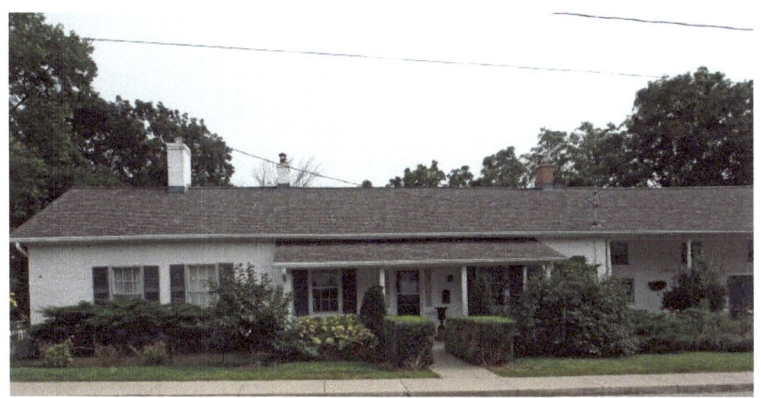

Grand River Street South

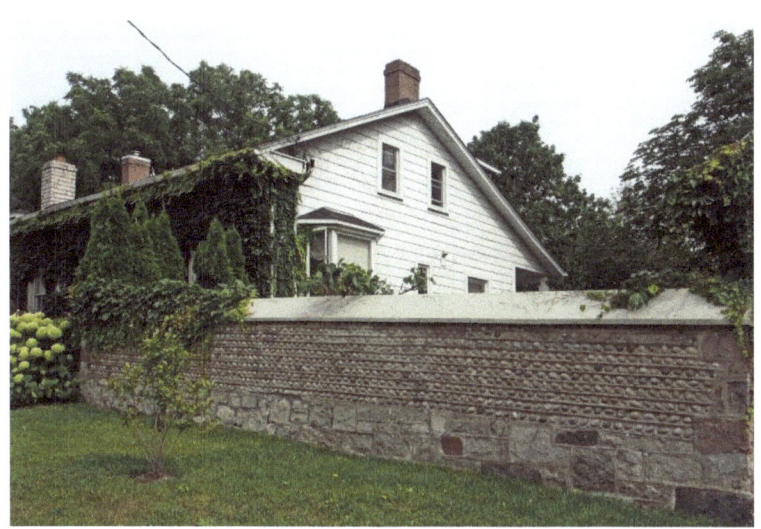

Cobblestone wall

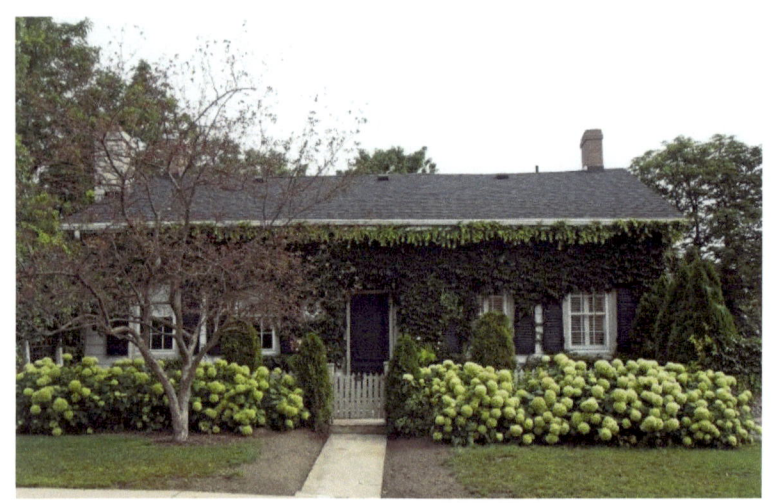

60 Grand River Street South

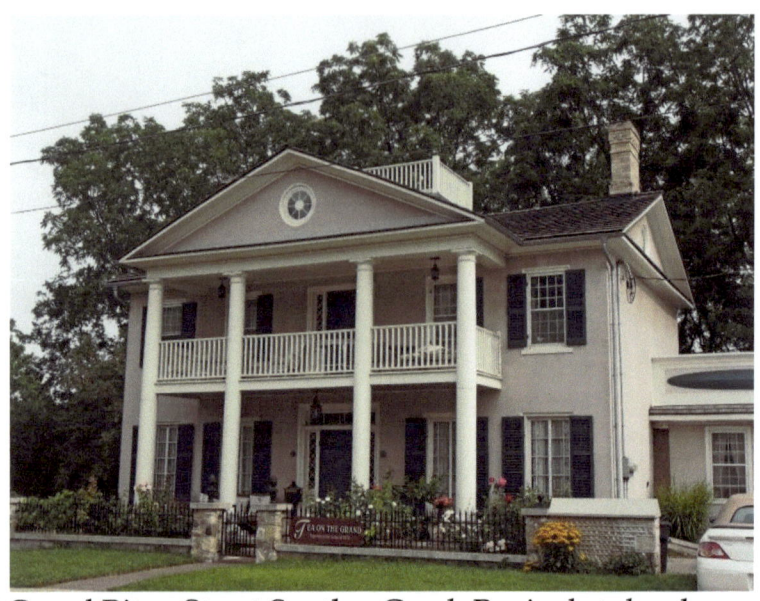

52 Grand River Street South – Greek Revival style – house of Asa Wolverton (sawmill owner), 1851 – wood frame construction covered in plaster of Paris

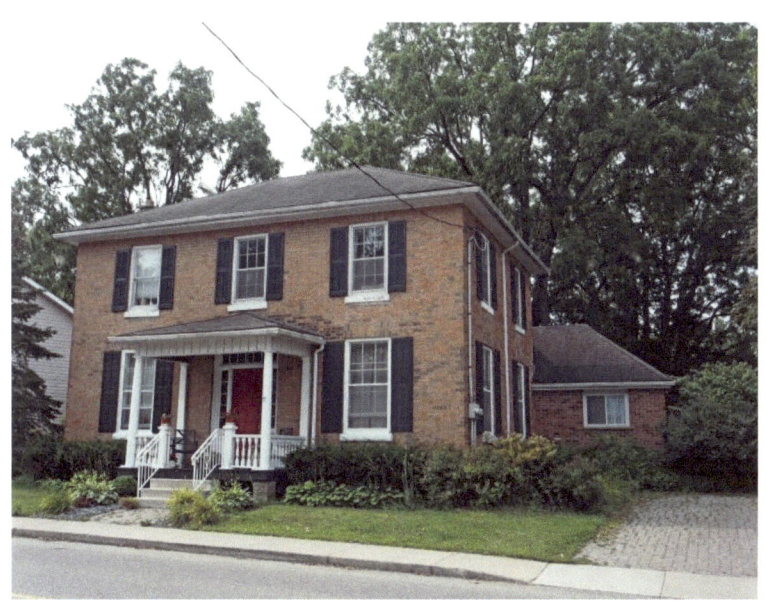

37 Grand River Street South – Georgian style, hipped roof

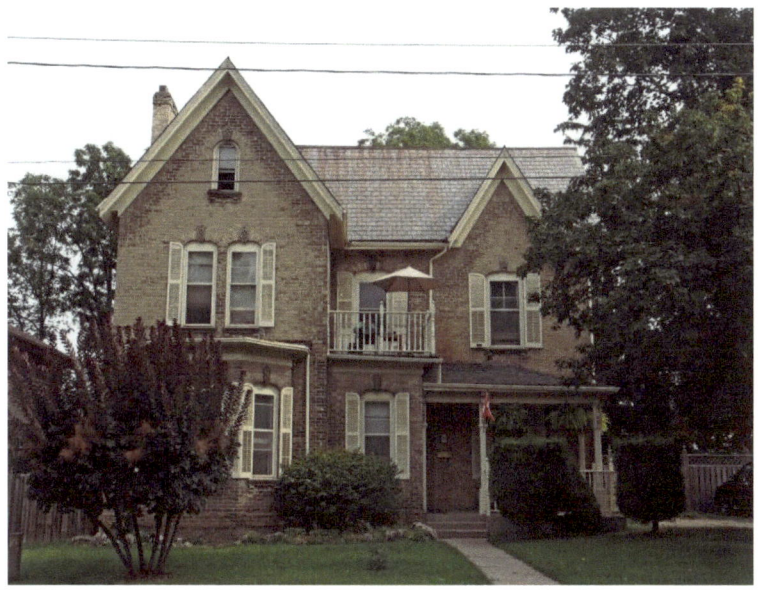

40 Grand River Street South – Gothic Revival, second floor balcony

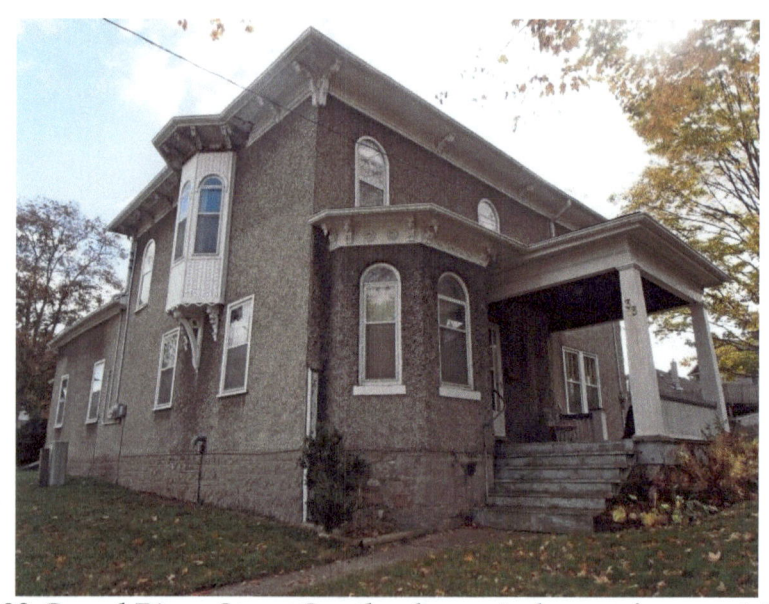

33 Grand River Street South – bay window at front, oriel window on side, cornice brackets

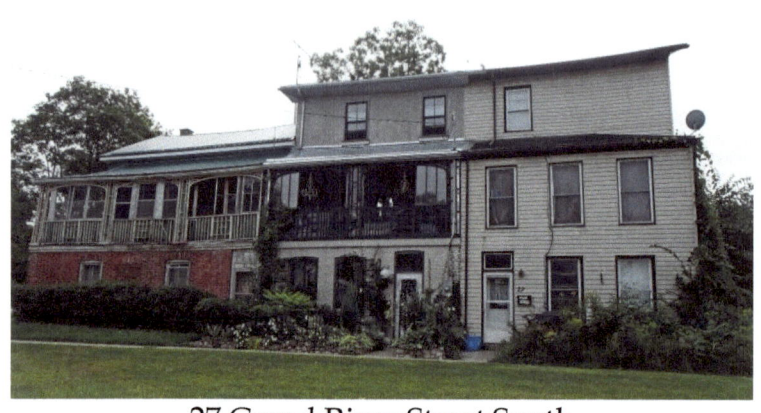

27 Grand River Street South

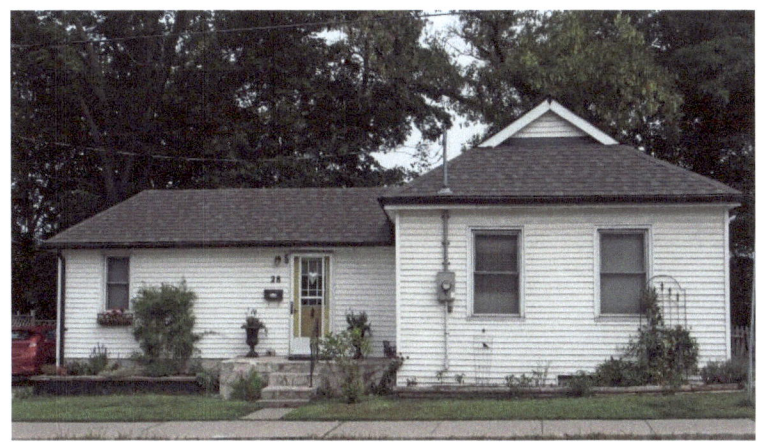

28 Grand River Street South

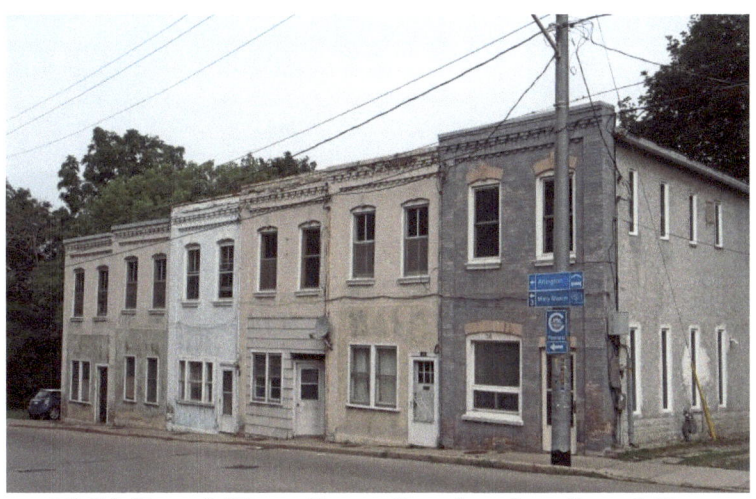

18-26 Grand River Street South – dentil molding

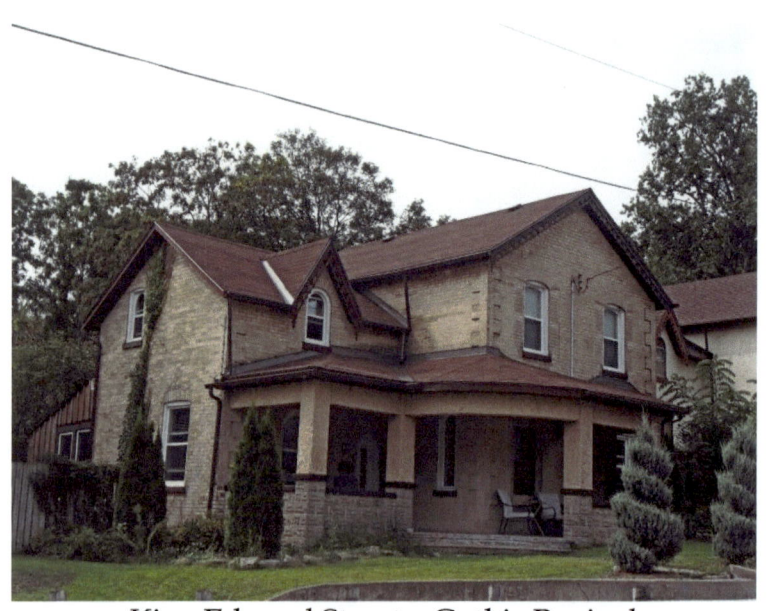

King Edward Street – Gothic Revival

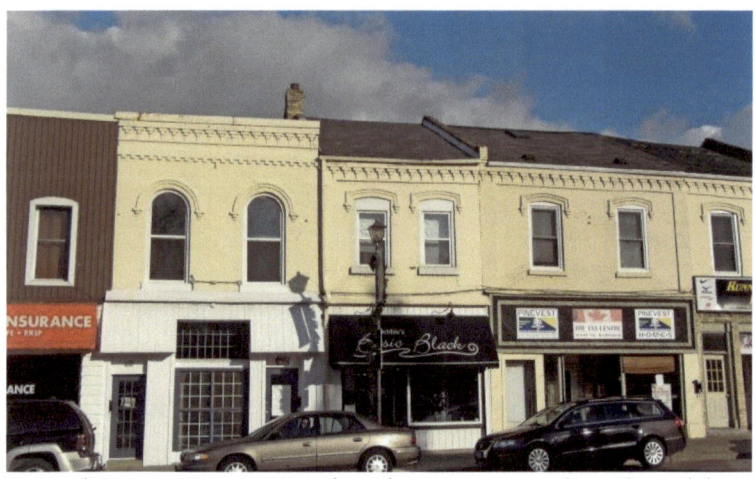

Grand River Street North - downtown - dentil molding

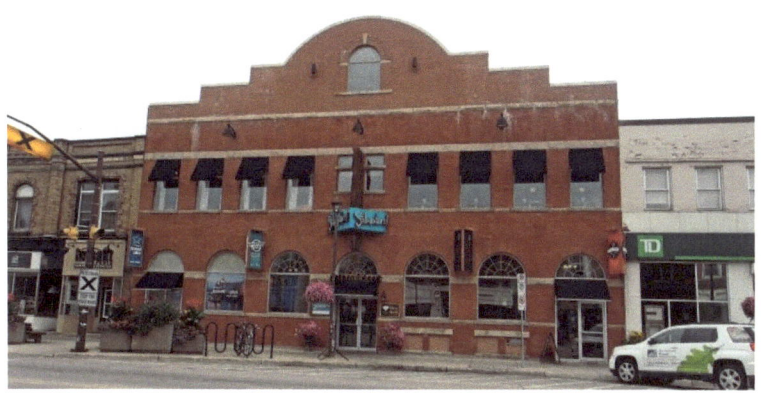

Grand River Street North - Downtown – storefront facades, stepped parapet, string courses

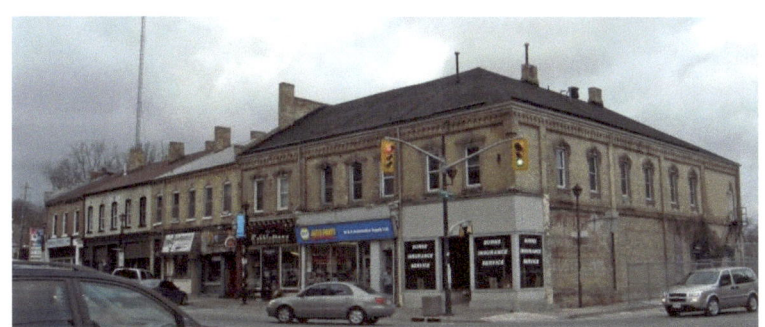

Hipped roof

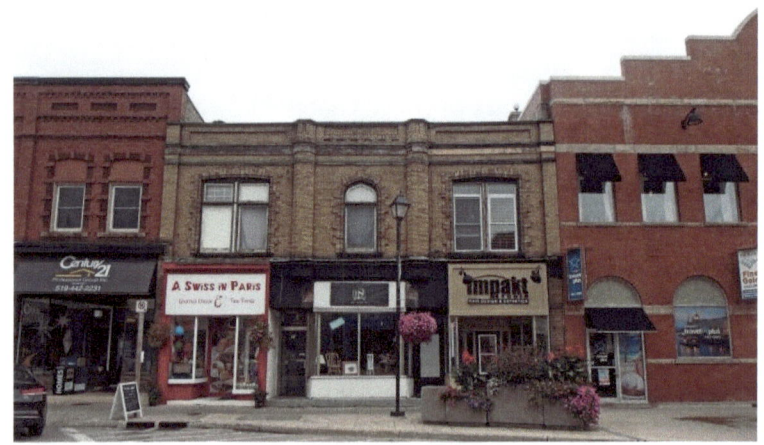

Grand River Street North - pilasters, string course

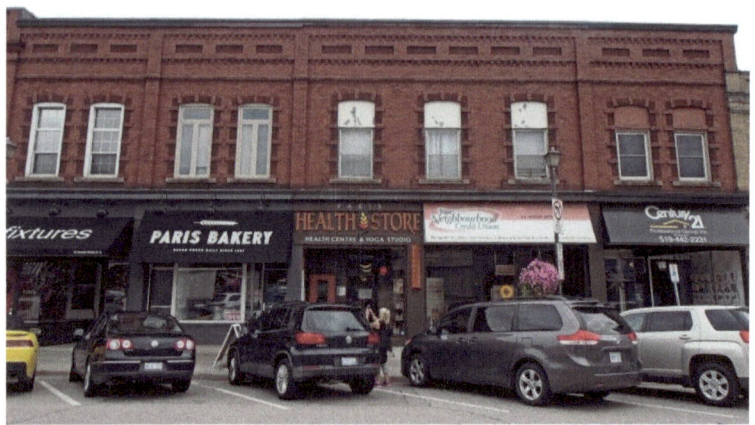

Grand River Street North - pilasters, bevelled dentil molding, decorative window surrounds, string courses

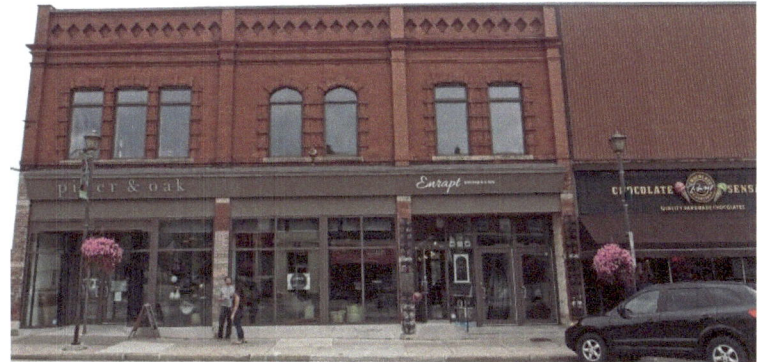

Grand River Street North - pilasters, decorative brick work

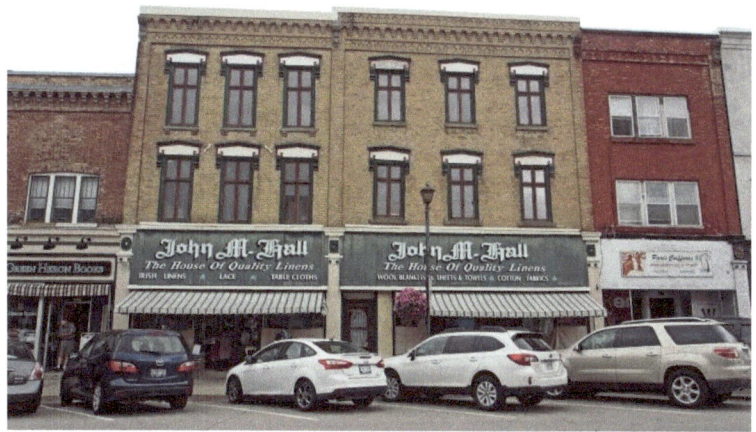

At Confederation, Thomas Hall was the proprietor of the local dry goods store. Generations later, John M. Hall, The House of Quality Linens at 43 Grand River Street continues the family tradition. Pilasters, decorative brick work, bevelled dentil molding.

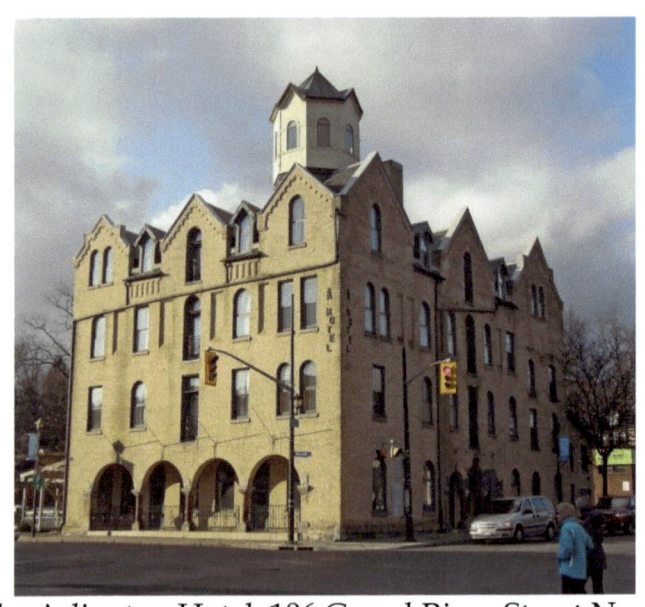

The Arlington Hotel, 106 Grand River Street North
c. 1850s, 1888 – 4-storey stucco and yellow brick reminiscent of the Chateau style, Romanesque style arcades supported by red-brown marble columns at the street level, octagonal tower, arched and rectangular windows

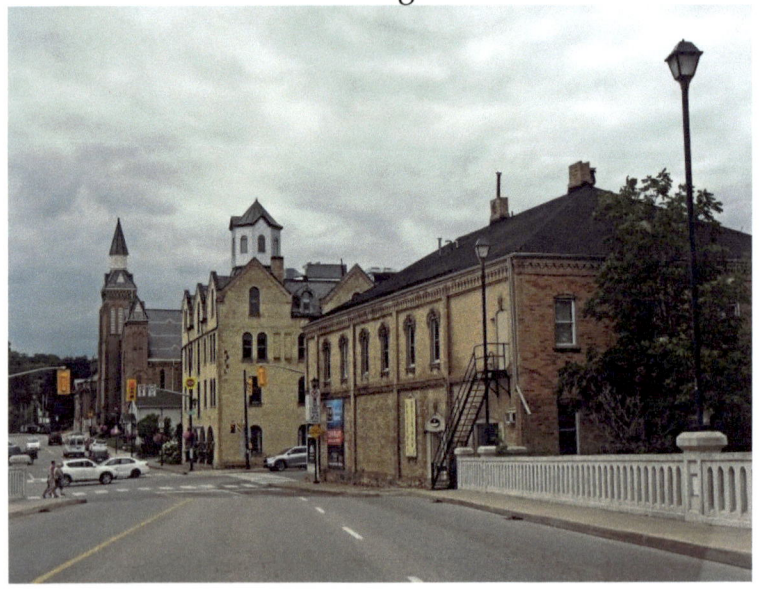

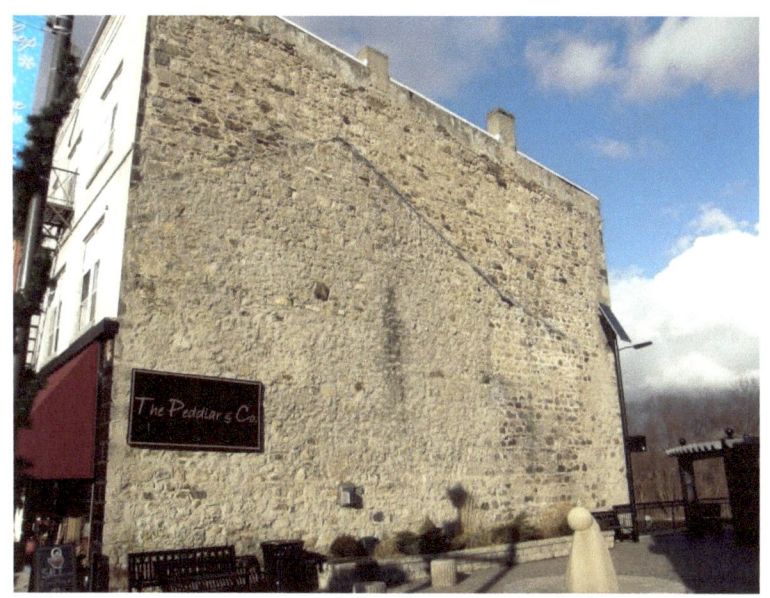

33 Grand River Street North – The Peddlar – rough cobblestone building

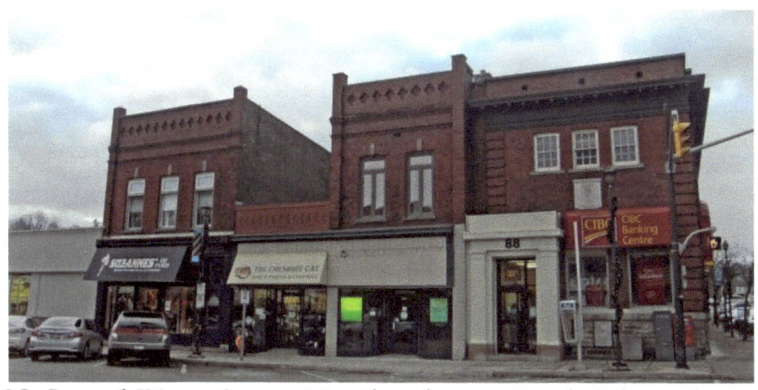

80-88 Grand River Street North - decorative brickwork, string courses, voussoirs and keystones

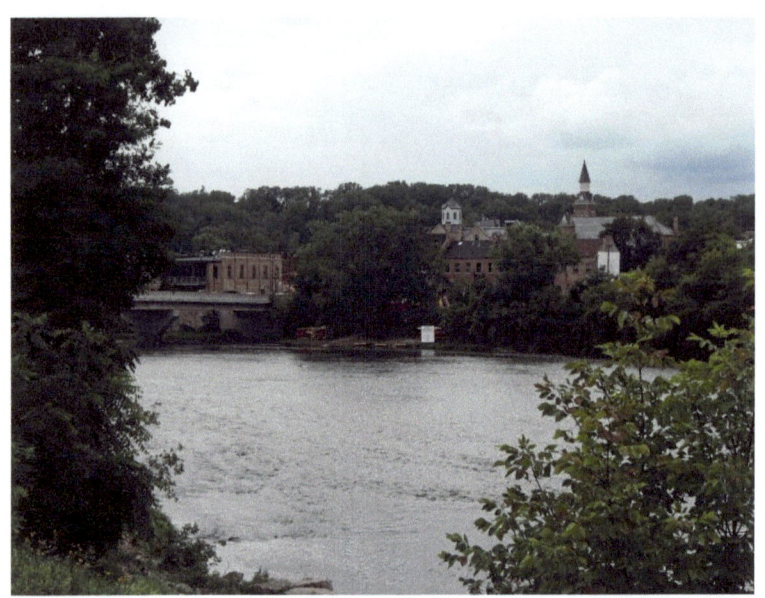

Grand River

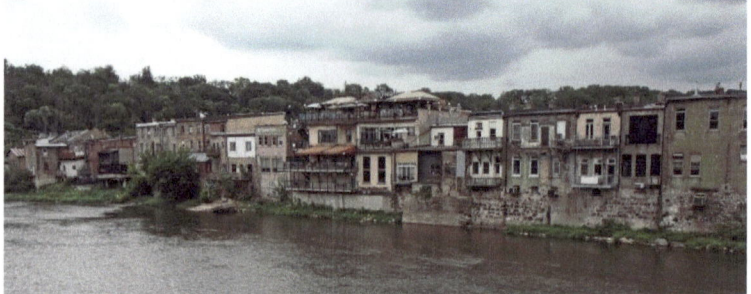

Buildings on the Grand River

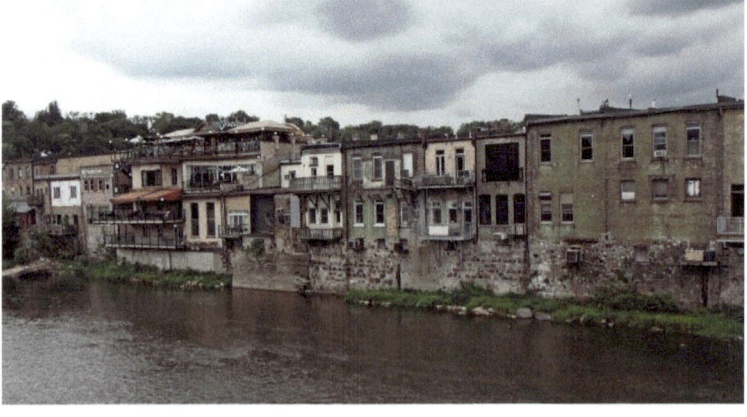

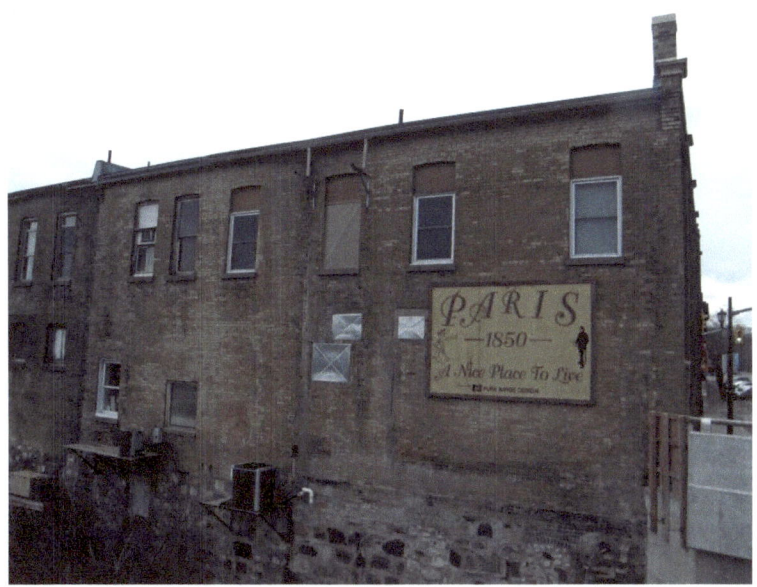
Cobblestone buildings on the waterfront

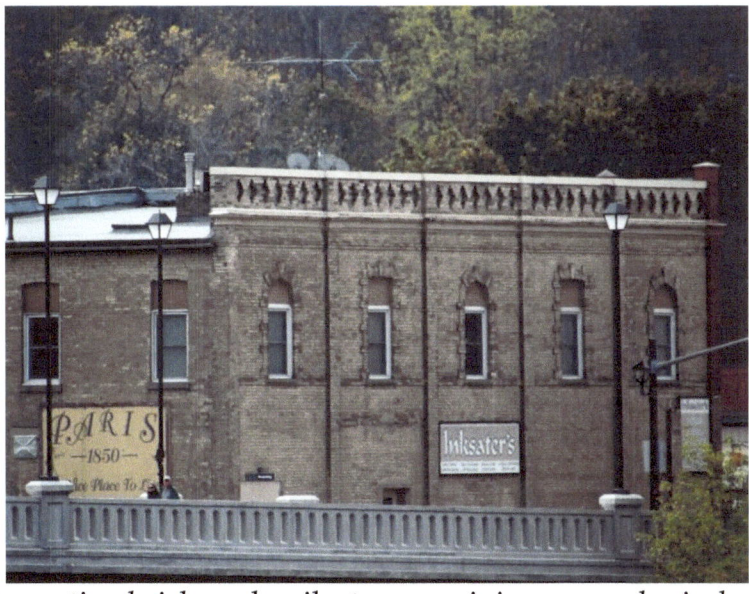
Decorative brickwork, pilasters, quoining around windows

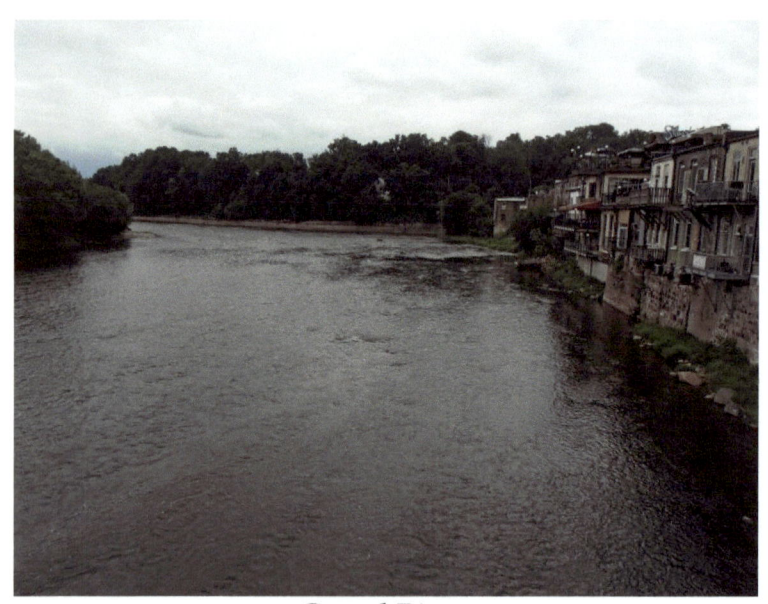

Grand River

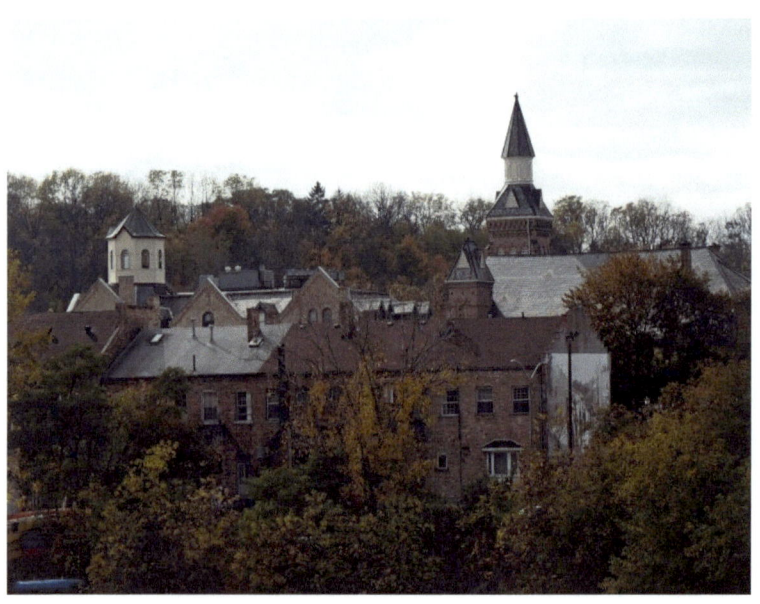

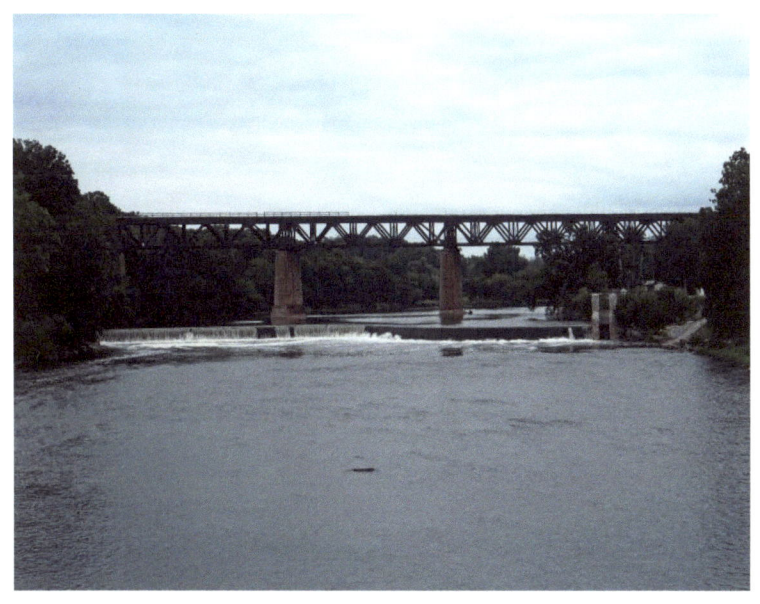

Railway Bridge across the Grand River

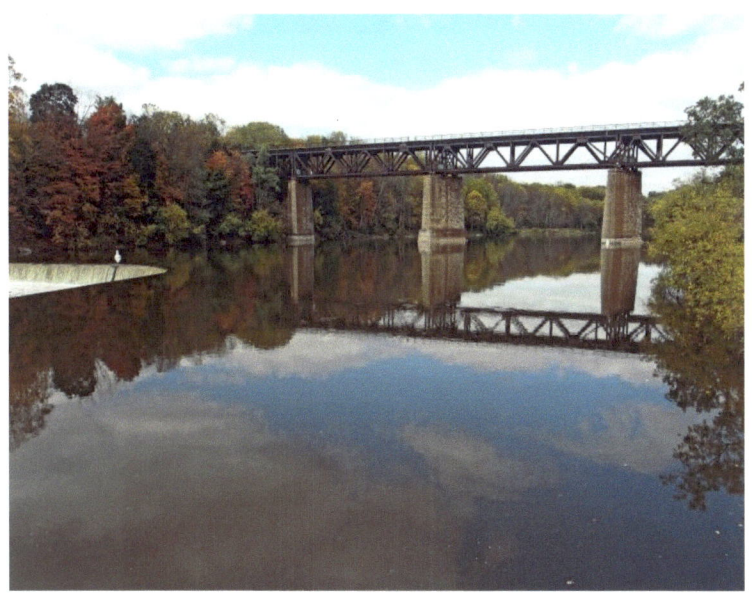

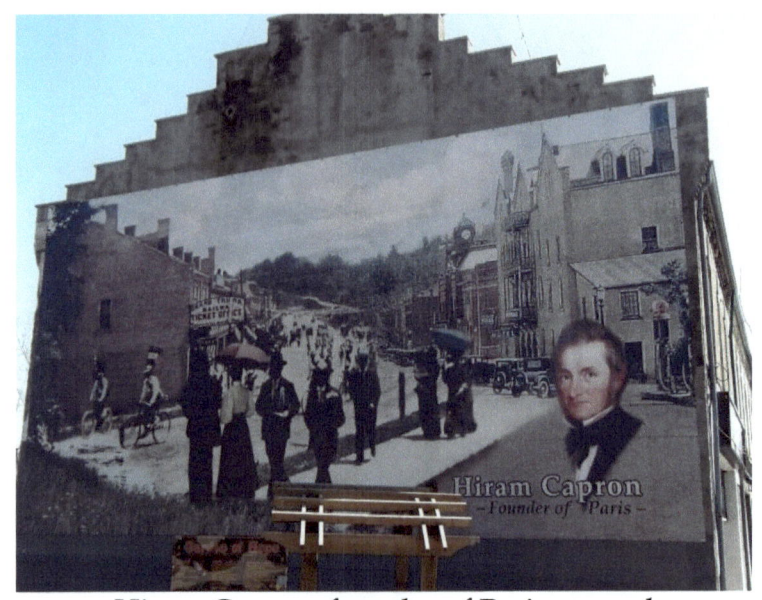

Hiram Capron, founder of Paris - mural

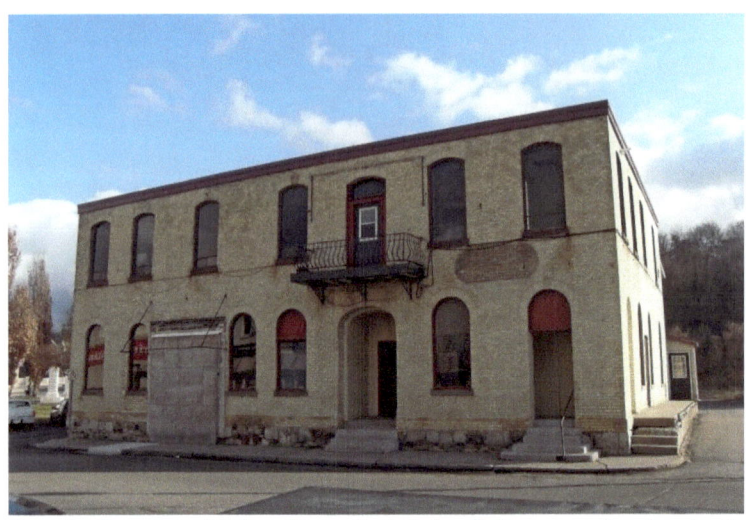

Mechanic Street - Old yellow brick building, arched windows, iron cresting for second floor balcony

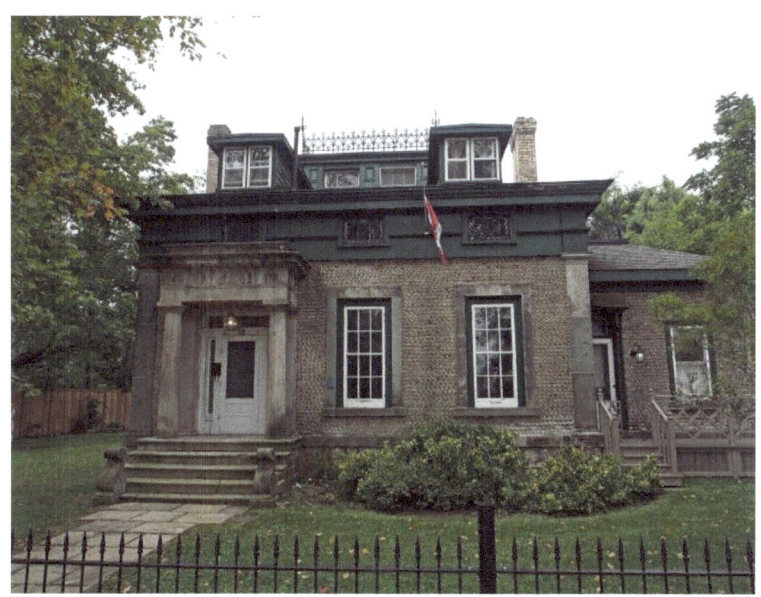

16 Broadway Street West – cobblestone masonry in the Greek Revival style was built in 1845. Cast iron grills cover "stomacher" windows beneath the eaves. A well-matched addition in 1885 housed a doctor's office. Smooth stones lintels and sills; the cobblestones are tilted; Greek symbols on the portico; dormers in attic; iron cresting on roof.

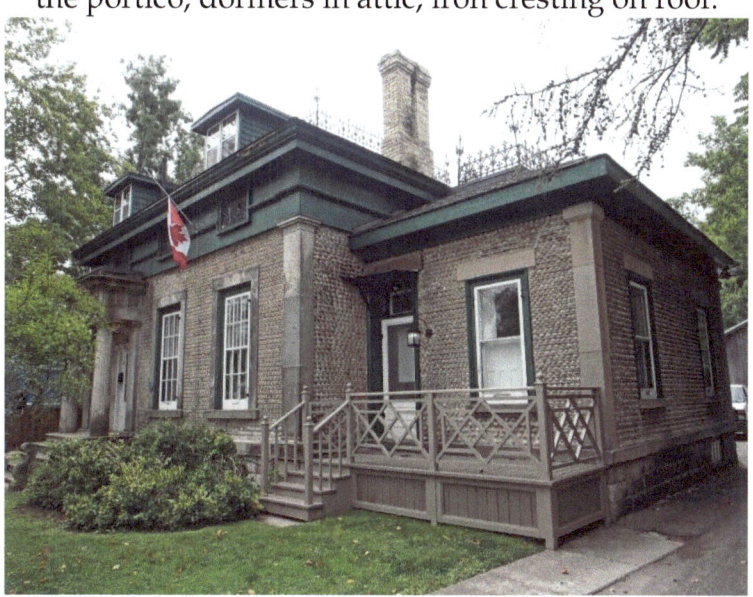

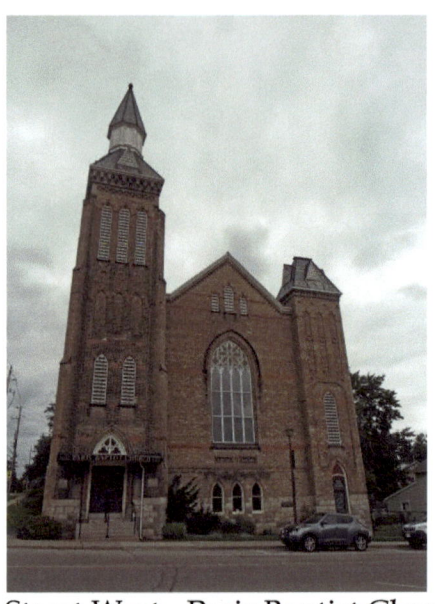

25 Broadway Street West - Paris Baptist Church – Gothic – built in 1885

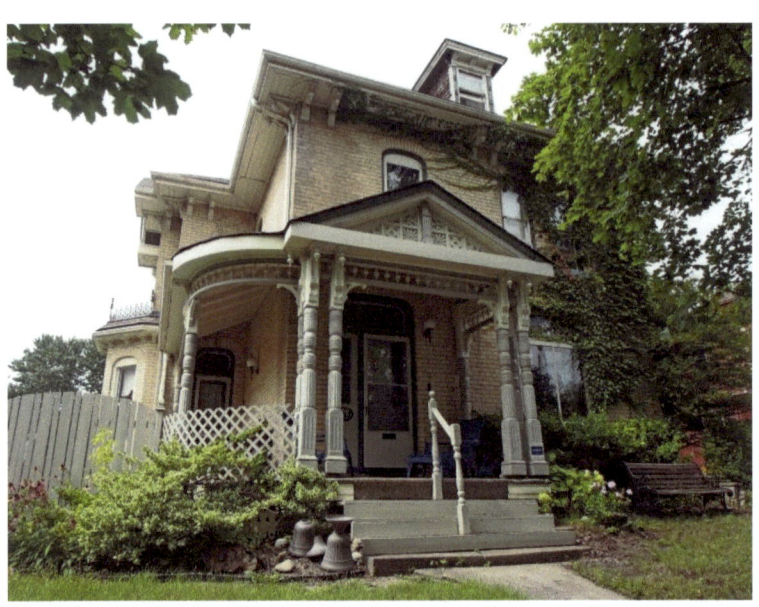

28 Broadway Street West – Italianate, dormer in attic, cornice brackets, turned porch supports, pediment

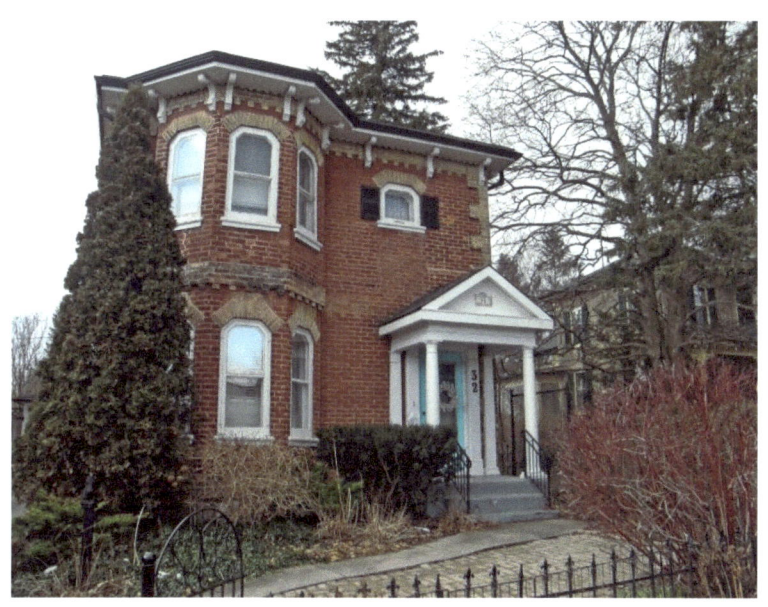

32 Broadway Street West - Italianate, cornice brackets, corner quoins, two-storey bay window, pediment above porch

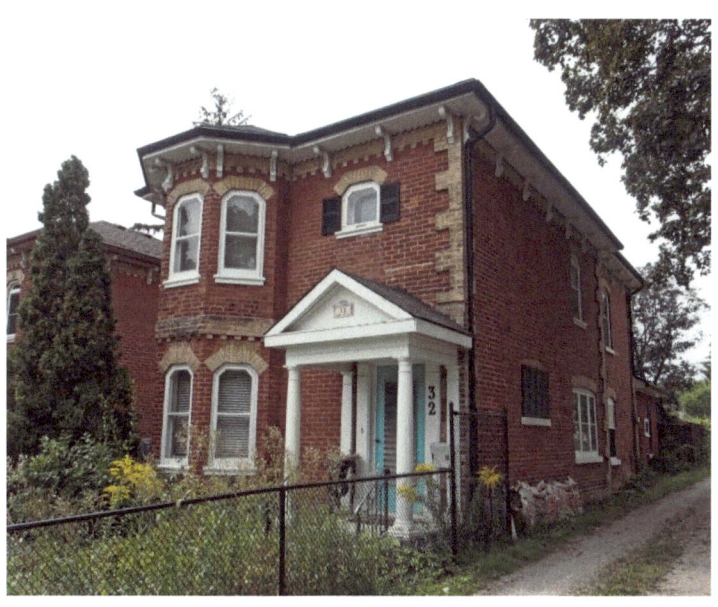

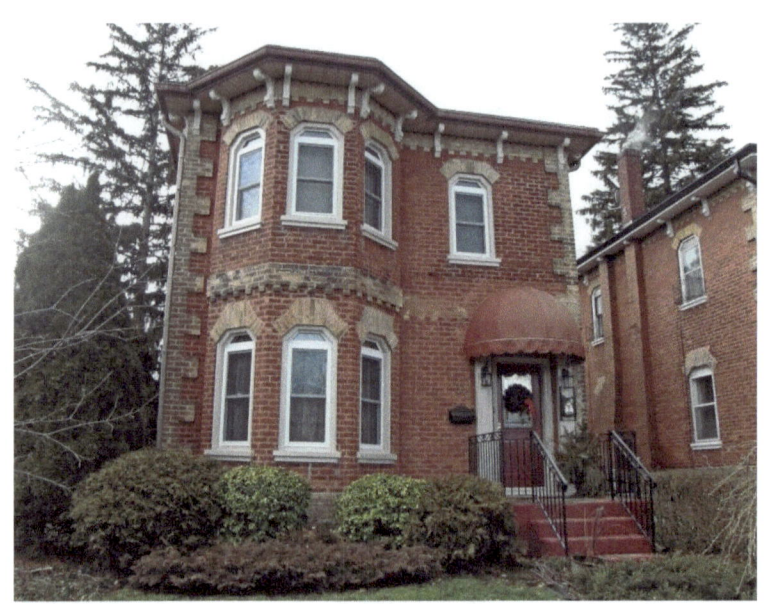

30 Broadway Street West – Italianate, cornice brackets, corner quoins, two-storey bay window

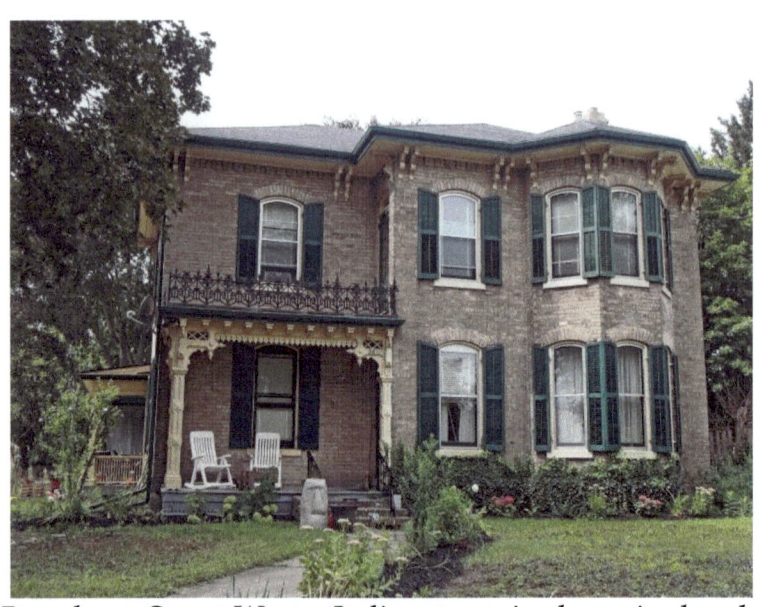

36 Broadway Street West – Italianate, paired cornice brackets, iron cresting on second floor balcony, two-storey bay window

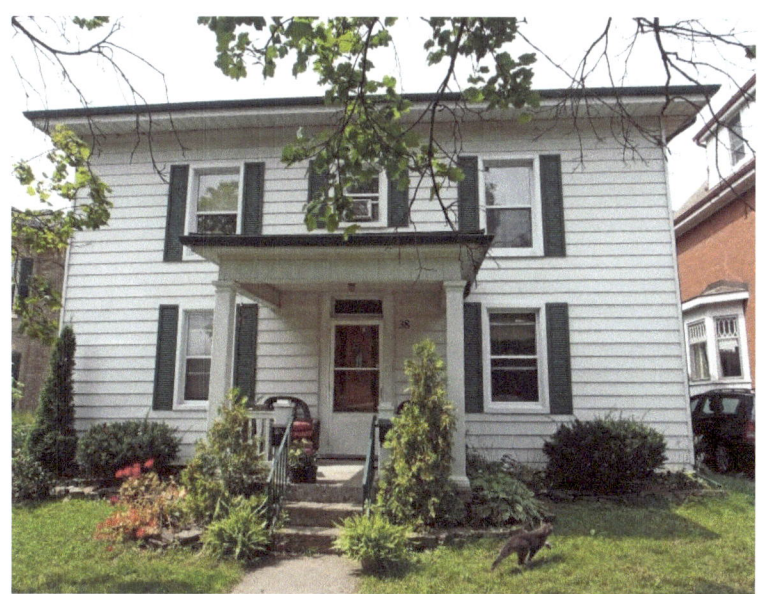

38 Broadway Street West - Georgian

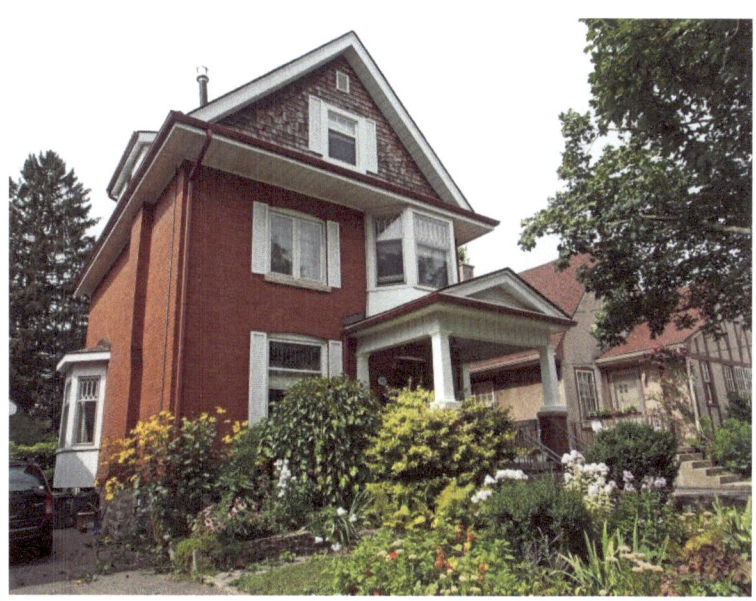

40 Broadway Street West – Edwardian, bay window on side, pediment above porch

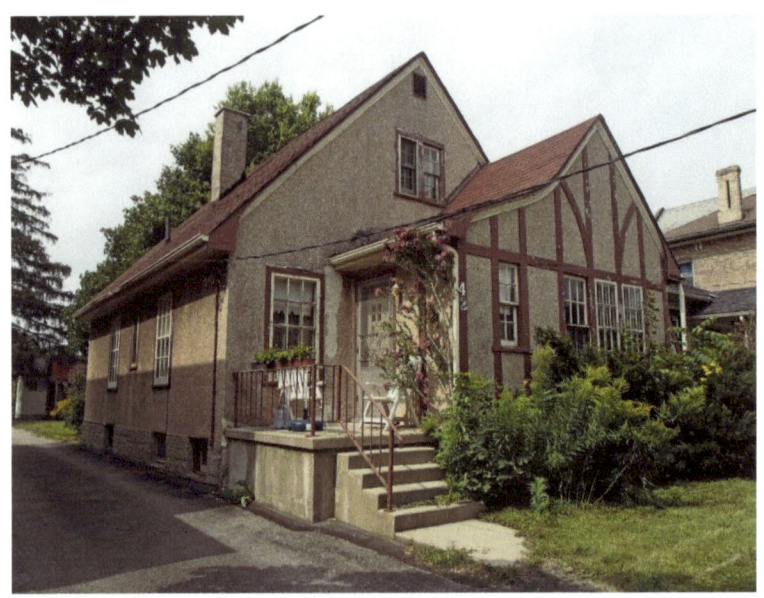

42 Broadway Street West – Tudor style stucco house

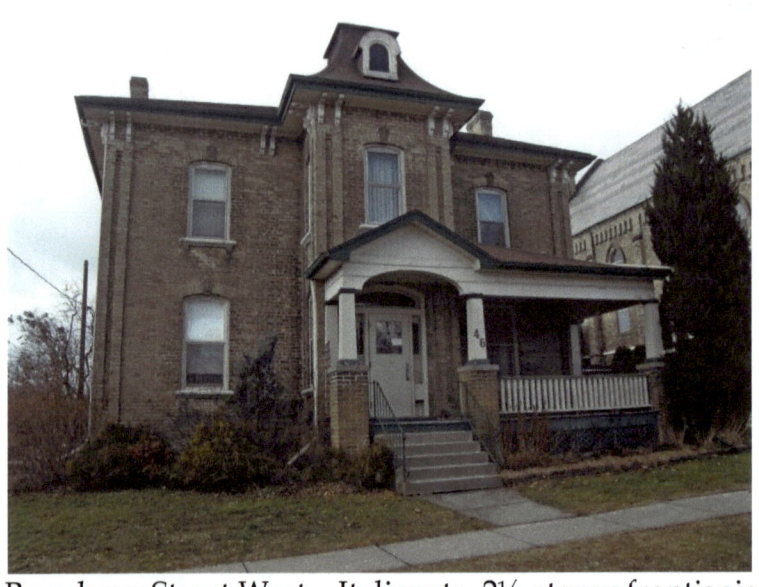

46 Broadway Street West – Italianate, 2½-storey frontispiece, voussoirs and keystones

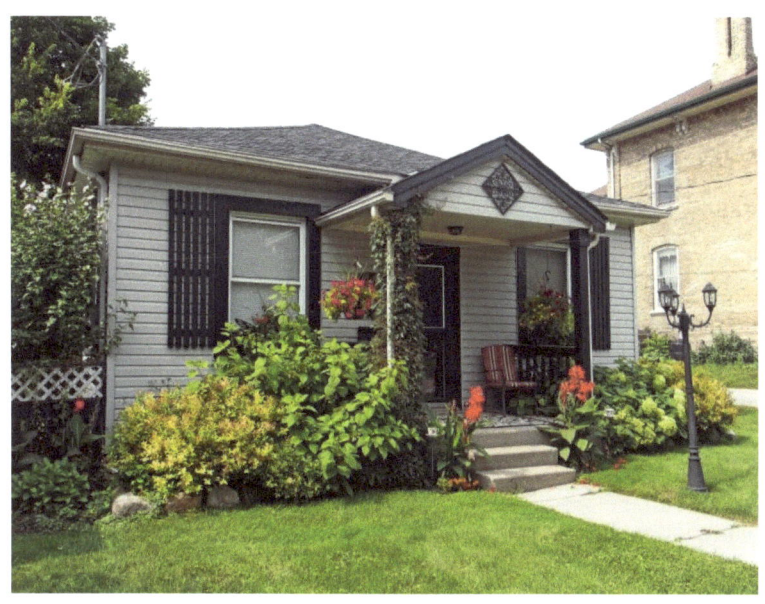

44 Broadway Street West – Teacups are ready – on stands on either side of the steps

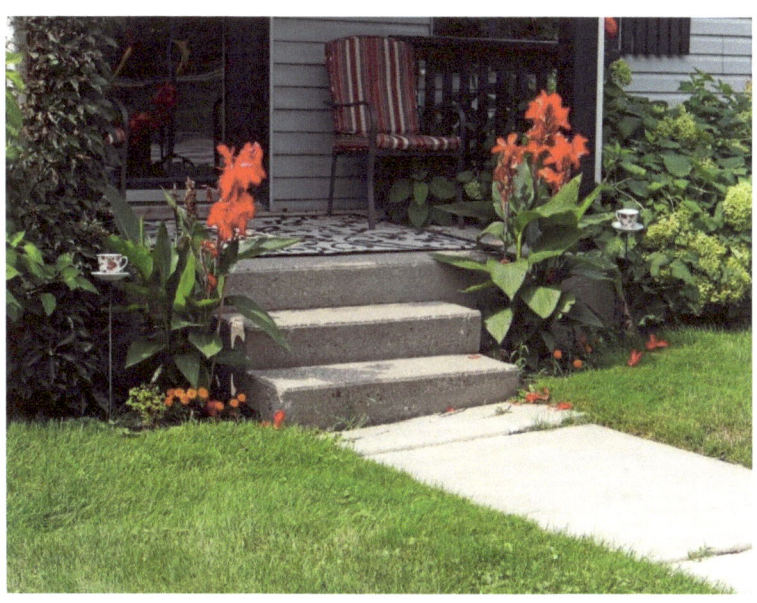

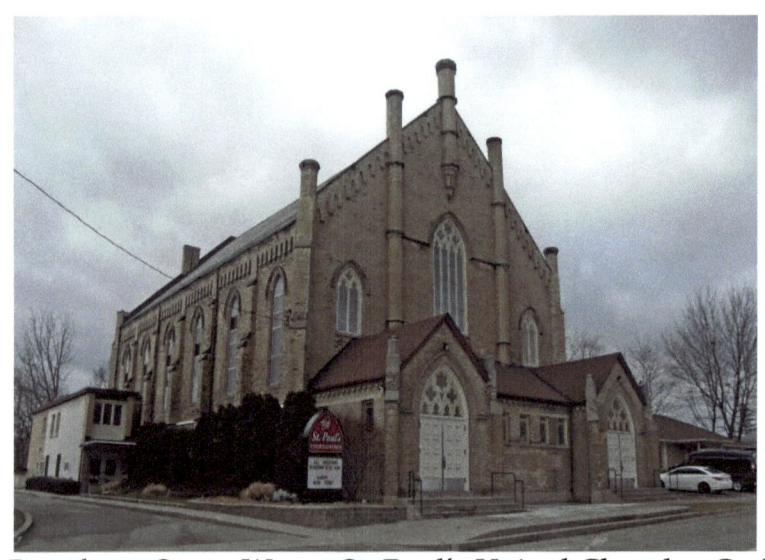

48 Broadway Street West – St. Paul's United Church – Gothic Revival, buttresses, bevelled dentil molding, muntins on windows, quatrefoils

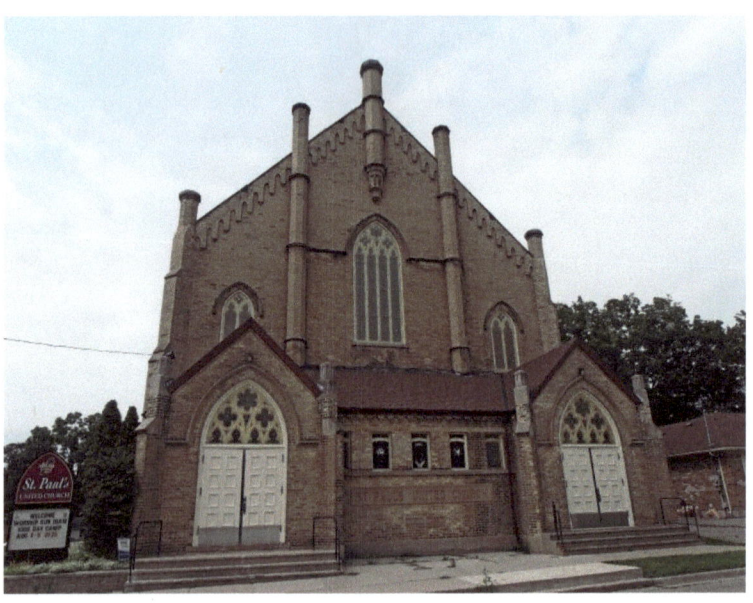

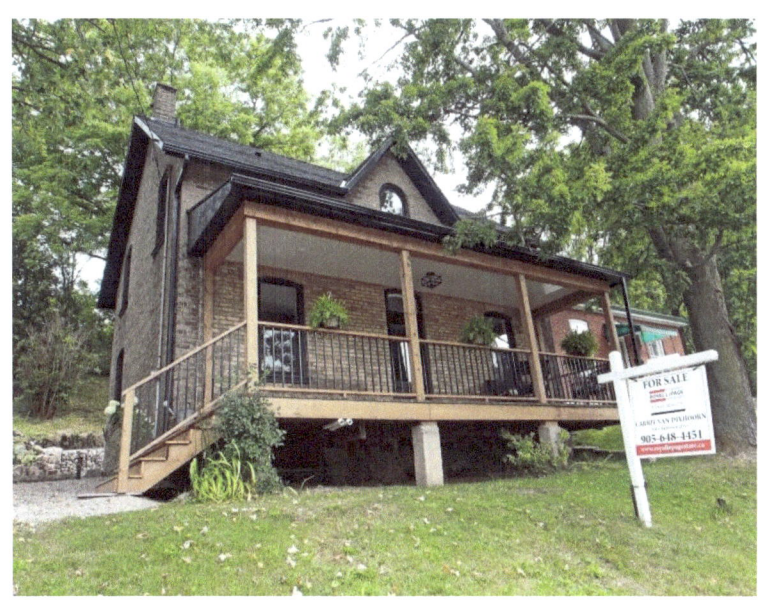

Broadway Street West - Gothic

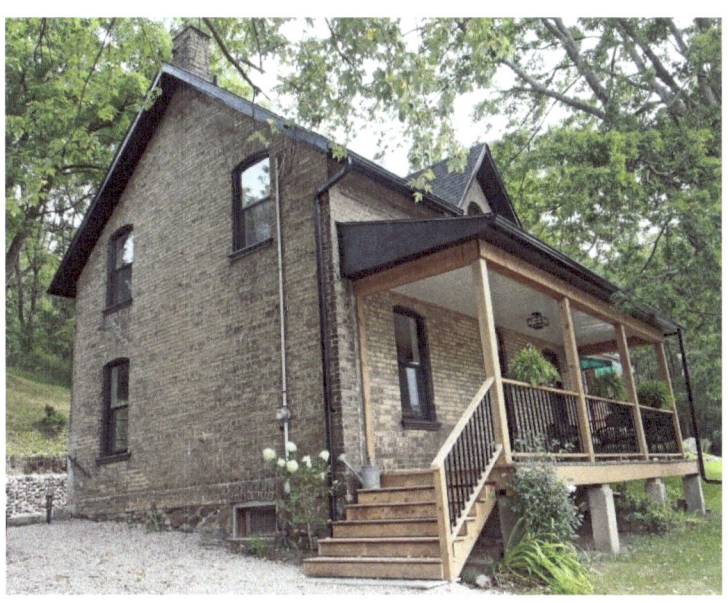

Architectural Terms

Brackets: a decorative or weight-bearing structural element which forms a right angle with one side against a wall and the other under a projecting surface such as an eave or roof. Example: 27 Dumfries Street, Page 21	
Buttress: a masonry structure built against or projecting from a wall which serves to support or reinforce the wall. In Canadian architecture, they are sometimes used for decoration. Example: Sacred Heart Church, 17 Washington Street, Page 24	
Cobblestone architecture: Refers to the use of cobblestones embedded in mortar as a method for erecting walls on houses and commercial buildings. Example: 19 Queen Street, Page 29	
Cornice Return: decorative element on the end of a gable. Example: 27 Dumfries Street, Page 21	
Dentil Moulding: an even series of rectangles used as ornamental decoration in cornices. Example: Grand River Street North, Page 44	

Dichromatic brickwork: the use of two colours of brick, tile or slate to decorate a façade. Example: Steeple on Sacred Heart Church, 17 Washington Street, Page 24	
Dormer: (French for "sleep") a gable end window that pierces through the plane of a sloping roof surface to create usable space in the top floor or attic of a building by adding headroom. Example: 57 Main Street, Page 23	
Frontispiece: a portion of the façade of a building, usually a centred doorway that is slightly raised from the rest of the building, usually with extensive ornamentation. Frontispieces are usually Classical in design with white columned porches. Example: 46 Broadway Street West, Page 60	
Gable: the triangular portion of a wall between the edges of a sloping roof. Example: 73 Grand River Street South, Page 36	
Hipped Roof: a roof where all sides slope downwards to the walls with no gables. Example: 39 Dumfries Street, Page 18	

Iron Cresting: A decorative ornament along the top of a roof. Iron cresting was popular in the Baroque era and also in Italianate, Victorian, Second Empire and Queen Anne styles of architecture. Example: 30 Dumfries Street, Page 17	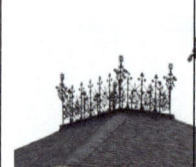
Keystones and Voussoirs: a voussoir is a wedge-shaped element used in building an arch. A keystone is the central stone that locks all the stones into position, allowing the arch to bear weight. A keystone is often enlarged and embellished. Example: 30 Broadway Street West, Page 58	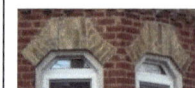
Lancet Window: a tall, narrow window with a pointed arch at its top. Example: 17 Washington Street, Page 24	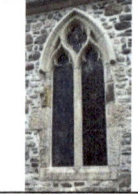
Lunette: A semi-circular area formed by an arch. Lunettes can either be windows or decorated areas at the end of a barrel vault. The windows were popular in Neo-classical and Classic Revival architecture in the 18th and 19th centuries in Canada. Example: 17 Washington Street, Page 24	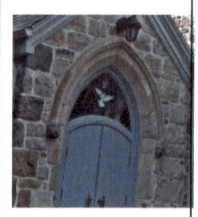

Muntin: When a window unit has more than one pane, the material that separates the panes is called the muntin. The larger, more decorative separations are called mullions. In stained glass windows, each piece of colored glass is held in place by a muntin. These were traditionally made of iron. Example: 17 Washington Street, Page 24	
Pediment: a triangular section above the horizontal structure (entablature), typically supported by columns. The inside of the triangle is called the tympanum. Example: 32 Broadway Street West, Page 57	
The **quatrefoil** is a type of decorative framework consisting of a symmetrical shape which forms the outline of four partially overlapping circles of the same diameter. The word quatrefoil comes from Latin and means "four leaves". Example: 48 Broadway Street West, Page 62	
Quoin: masonry blocks at the corner of a wall, often a decorative feature, usually larger or of a different colour than the rest of the wall. Example: 19 Queen Street, Page 29	

Building Styles

Edwardian, 1900-1930 – This style bridges the ornate and elaborate styles of the Victorian era and the simplified styles of the 20th century. Balanced facades, simple roof lines, dormer windows, large front porches, and smooth brick surfaces are its characteristics. Example: 73 Grand River Street South, Page 36	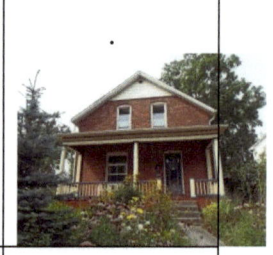
Georgian, before 1860 – This style began with the British King Georges in the 18th century. These buildings have balanced facades around a central door, medium-pitched gable roofs, and small paned windows. Example: 40 Dumfries Street, Page 18	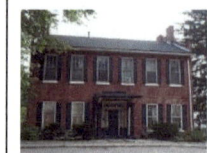
Gothic Revival, 1830-1890 – These decorative buildings have sharply-pitched gables with highly detailed verge boards, pointed-arch window openings, and dichromatic brickwork. It is a common style in Ontario. Example: 40 Grand River Street South, Page 41	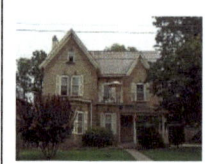

Greek Revival – have gabled or hipped roofs with low pitches. The cornice of the main roof usually has a wide band which represents the entablature of classical Greek architecture consisting of the frieze and the architrave. Greek or Roman columns usually support the porch. The front door is surrounded by sidelights and a rectangular transom and is usually dressed with pilasters, pediments and/or columns. Example: 52 Grand River Street South, Page 40	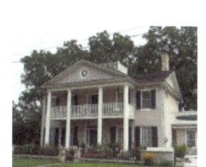
Italianate, 1850-1900 – It has wide-bracketed eaves, belvederes, wrap-around verandahs. Example: 30 Broadway Street West, Page 58	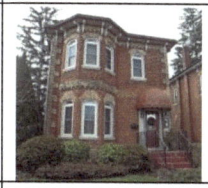
Queen Anne, 1885-1900 – This style is distinguished by an irregular outline featuring a combination of an offset tower, broad gables, projecting two-storey bays, verandahs, multi-sloped roofs, and tall, decorative chimneys. A mixture of brick and wood is common. Windows often have one large single-paned bottom sash and small panes in the upper sash. Example: 22 Church Street, Page 14	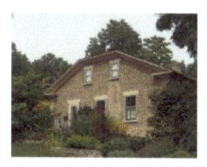 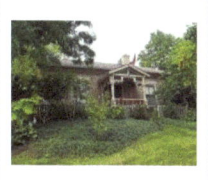

Regency Cottage, 1830-1860 – This style originated in England in 1815 and spread to Ontario later in the 19th century as British officers retired to Canada. It is a modest one-storey house with a low-pitched hip roof and has a symmetrical front façade. Example: 57 Main Street, Page 23	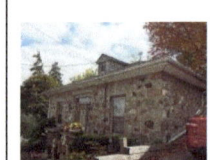
Tudor Revival – exposed timbers with stucco infill, multi-paned windows. Example: 42 Broadway Street West, Page 60	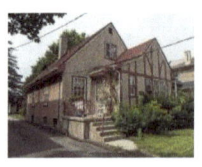

www.ingramcontent.com/pod-product-compliance
Lightning Source LLC
Chambersburg PA
CBHW041941240526
45473CB00033B/191